You've Gotta Gotta Hand It to God!

Timothy M. Powell

Radiant BOOKS

Gospel Publishing House/Springfield, Mo. 65802

02-0859

Library of Congress Catalog Card Number 84-73557
International Standard Book Number 0-88243-859-X
Printed in the United States of America

Contents

1

Anchored or Adrift?

"I'm fed up! I've had just about all of this place I can handle. 'Do this! Stop that! Watch this! Carry that over there! Stack this down here! Stand up! Sit down! Feed the animals! Clean the stables!' I've taken just about all the orders I'm going to! I think it's time I got out on my own. I hate the way this place is being run; it'd sure be different if I were in charge. And since I'm not, I guess it's time to clear out. Make it on my own. Do things *my* way. It'd be fun to manage my own life for a change, instead of having everybody else tell me what to do all the time," so the young man reasoned to himself.

Before long, he got up the courage to carry out his scheme. He went to his father, asked for his inheritance, and struck out on his own. What a relief he felt to be out on his own! No more rules and regulations. No more restrictions on how he had to live or how he could spend his money.

Finally, he had some freedom, and he fully intended to make it big in the world.

But one day—while he was working at his new job—he sat down to take inventory: "Wow, I've had some great times! Those parties I gave and those other ones I went to—they were fantastic. There sure were some great lookin' girls there, and, ooohh, the food . . . the food was out of this world. What I wouldn't give for a bite of that food right now! I'm so hungry—so hungry that even this slop I have to give the pigs smells good. I wonder . . . I wonder what the servants that work for my father are eating right now."

Things hadn't run as smoothly as he'd thought they would. It wasn't as easy to manage the affairs of life as the young man once imagined. "Maybe all those orders and rules and regulations weren't so crazy after all. I don't seem to have done all that well without them." What was the answer? There was only one, if he wanted to keep from dying: return to his father's house and ask to be accepted as a servant, go back where sound management principles provided abundance even for the slaves. So the young man set out.

But even before he got all the way back home, his father spotted him. Out of the house he ran to greet his son, hugged him, rejoiced over his return, and began a celebration. And instead of making him merely a slave, the Father reinstated him as a full son, lavishing upon him all the benefits that go along with sonship. With his father's help, that young man was able to get his life back in order, because he'd returned to the place where sound management principles were practiced.

The Scriptural Steward

Did that story sound familiar? Most likely it did. It was a freewheeling retelling of one of Jesus' parables, the Parable of the Prodigal Son in Luke 15. So what's the point? Simply this, the life of the runaway son illustrates for us the choices each person faces in the area of stewardship. The most common choice is to go after all the funds, fantasy, and fun the world has to offer. But how often that route leads to disillusionment, even to despair and suffering.

The Bible teaches, on the other hand, that the real Christian steward is a person who's been promoted from service in the sty of the world and sin and Satan to service in the household of God. In fact, the New Testament word for *steward* means "manager of the house." The Christian steward enters God's household, and to serve as a manager in that household, he has to submit to the rules of the "Boss." It's a matter of establishing a stable economy, something that can be done only under the direction of the "Master Economist." It's interesting that our English word *economy* derives from the New Testament term for *stewardship.* The way you manage, organize, arrange, and run the household of your life— that's scriptural economics. And that's Christian stewardship.

Improve Your Economy

Problems run rampant with national economics. Daily we read in the newspapers, hear on the six o'clock news, of inflation, recession, depression, recovery—they're all familiar terms. On the national and international level, economy means money: debts, surpluses, shortages, deficits. The key concern of our leaders: How can we improve the economy? How can we prop it up so it doesn't topple over on us?

Money is important in scriptural economics too. Christian stewardship demands careful money management. Jesus often taught about money. But genuine Christian stewardship involves every area of life. The economy of nature has to do with the relationships and interactions of all the parts of the world around us. That's what New Testament economics is all about. It's a total system, not just a matter of money. Actions, attitudes, abilities, desires, relationships, time—these and a host of other matters are the concerns of Christian stewardship. Money is among them, but it's only a small part of the system. Christians have to commit themselves to improve their entire economy. That's what scriptural stewardship is all about. "You are not your own; you were bought at a price" (1 Corinthians 6:19,20, NIV).

The Basics

Have you ever heard of a football coach who didn't know the rules of football? Or a builder who knew nothing about construction? How about a truck driver who never learned to drive? Not too likely. But what about a Christian steward who knew nothing about Christian stewardship? A football coach can't be effective unless he knows the rules. A builder can't build if he doesn't know how. A truck driver who never learned to drive is headed for a crash. And a Christian who knows nothing about Christian stewardship travels just as dangerously.

The basics. You've got to know the basics. Without the basics, you're like a ship adrift—blown about by every breeze that arises. To hold steady throughout the storm, a ship's got to be anchored to something secure, something that won't give way no matter how rough the seas.

The Christian steward is bound to be battered if he floats aimlessly on life's sea. He needs an anchor—something to hold him firm and steady. The Bible provides that mooring place. Its principles endure, unshaken by the tests of time and the trials of circumstances. The Christian steward must be anchored to the principles of Scripture, otherwise he'll drift amidst a sea of overwhelming, worldly theories. "Know the basics! Get the fundamentals!" That's what my coaches always said. You've got to do that before you can develop as an athlete, and you've got to do that before you can serve as a faithful Christian steward.

Jesus and the Fundamentals

What are the fundamentals of stewardship? What are those mooring points that I can tie on to and feel secure, knowing they won't erode and leave me adrift?

In Luke 19 Jesus tells of a well-to-do man who had to be absent from his estate for a period of time so that he could travel to a far land and officially be proclaimed king. Before his departure, he called 10 of his servants and gave each one a pound, which was the equivalent of about 3 months' wages. His orders: " 'Put this money to work . . . until I come back' " (v. 13, NIV).

The man was proclaimed king, in spite of the complaints of his subjects, and when he returned to his estate, he called for the servants who had been given charge of his money. One fellow had multiplied his amount 10 times over, returning 10 pounds in place of the one he had been allotted. A second returned five in place of the one. Both of these men were commended and promoted in their level of service to the new king.

A third servant came: "Lord, behold, here is thy pound, which I have kept laid up in a napkin: for I feared thee, because thou art an austere man: thou takest up that thou layedst not down, and reapest that thou didst not sow" (vv. 20,21).

The king responded with harsh words: "Out of thine own mouth will I judge thee, thou wicked servant. Thou knewest that I was an austere man, taking up that I laid not down, and reaping that I did not sow: wherefore then gavest not thou my money into the bank, that at my coming I might have required mine own with usury? And he said unto them that stood by, Take from him the pound, and give it to him that hath ten pounds" (vv. 22-24).

The Real Owner

Christ's Parable of the Pounds emphasizes a very important truth, a truth that's taught throughout the Bible: God is the owner of all there ever was, is, and ever will be. That's a fact you need to tie on to. It's one of those anchors that will keep you from drifting. Listen to some verses that make this principle crystal clear: "Behold, the heaven and the heaven of heavens is the Lord's thy God, the earth also, with all that therein is" (Deuteronomy 10:14). "The earth is the Lord's, and the fulness thereof; the world, and they that dwell therein" (Psalm 24:1). "The earth is the Lord's, and the fulness thereof" (1 Corinthians 10:26).

Here are a few more passages to read: Exodus 9:29; 19:5; 1 Chronicles 29:11; Job 41:11; Psalm 50:12; Daniel 4:25. And these are only a fraction of the verses in the Bible that teach God's ownership of all that exists. It is a principle abundantly maintained in Scripture. God is the Creator, the Sustainer, and the Owner of all that is.

Theodore Roosevelt National Park in western North Dakota is famous for its badlands, hills carved by water and wind into shapes of sheer beauty. But as I drive through those badlands, I am more astounded by the magnificent buffalo that roam those hills than by the hills themselves. They are truly awesome creatures. Each time I see one, however, I can't help but think back to when those beautiful animals were mercilessly slaughtered by ruthless hunters for the money they could make from their hides.

Why were the hunters able to slaughter the buffalo? Because no one owned those animals that roamed the plains in such tremendous numbers. They belonged to no one. So the hunters reasoned they could be abused and annihilated. That's exactly what happens when men lose sight of God's ownership of all that exists. Abuse and annihilation lurk nearby.

Back to the story Jesus told: The nobleman "called his ten servants, and delivered them ten pounds" (Luke 19:13). There's no question about *whose* money was being distributed. It certainly wasn't the servants'. No, it was the nobleman's money. The servants knew that full well. But how many Christians realize that whatever comes into their possession really belongs to God? He is the real owner.

Every Good Gift

"Every good gift and every perfect gift is from above, and cometh down from the Father of lights" (James 1:17). Not only is God the great Owner, He is also the great Giver. He is the Bestower of all goodness and abundance that comes your way.

The greatest example of God's giving nature is in John 3:16: "God so loved the world that he gave his only begotten Son." He gave the most precious gift of all when He gave His Son. God was the Initiator.

The nobleman "*called* his ten servants, and delivered them ten pounds" (Luke 19:13, emphasis mine). That's what God is like. He's the Initiator, the Giver. The servants didn't come and beg or badger the nobleman for money. Not at all! The master called them and gave them the money. What a picture of our God! All resources lie at His disposal. He bestows a portion on each one of us, not because we deserve it or because we're so good, but because He is so good.

No wonder Paul could ask the Christians in Corinth:

11

"What hast thou that thou didst not receive?"
(1 Corinthians 4:7). The answer then remains the answer
now. We have received nothing that was not given us
by God. He's the Owner and Giver of all we possess.
That's a fundamental of stewardship.

Christian Caretakers

I had to return to school for the summer and needed
an inexpensive place to stay. Some friends had planned
a vacation during that same time and generously offered
to allow me to "house sit" while they were away. I jumped
at the chance. A beautiful house, nice yard, no charge—
if I would just keep a careful eye on their home, attend
to the small necessities, and make sure no vandals broke
in to steal their possessions.

I took extra care during my stay not to spill anything
on the carpets, not to use too much electricity, to make
sure the lawn and flowers were well watered, weeded,
and trimmed. I cared deeply for those friends, and I felt
a responsibility to carry out my tasks to the best of my
ability. I was using and tending someone else's possessions. I had to be very careful.

That's precisely the responsibility we must assume
under God. We are caretakers, trustees of what really
belongs to God. In Christ's Parable of the Pounds, all
three of the servants clearly understood that the money
they had been given belonged not to them but to their
master and that they were responsible for its use. Even
the unprofitable servant knew that (see Luke 19:20,21).

Granted, not everyone accepts that responsibility. In
the parable, "some of [the master's] people hated him
and sent him their declaration of independence, stating
that they had rebelled and would not acknowledge him
as their king" (Luke 19:14, *The Living Bible*). That's also

a description of those who stubbornly refuse to acknowledge their responsibility as caretakers under God's lordship. But their stubbornness can't alter the facts. Luke 19:15 says the master was enthroned and proclaimed as king, in spite of their objections and protests.

It's no wonder Paul encouraged the Colossians with these words: "Whatsoever ye do, do it heartily, as to the Lord, and not unto men" (Colossians 3:23). The true Christian steward views all of life and everything he possesses as a responsibility granted him by God. Proper care, tender nurture, wise planning, cautious vigilance—these are the responsibilities of the steward, not because he fears God's heavy hand, but because he loves the great Giver!

Lessons From a Fishbowl

My sister and her family had left for several weeks on vacation. Seven-year-old Sharon's goldfish, Cleo, was left in the care of Ray, a close elderly friend. For more than 2 weeks Ray meticulously cared for Cleo, providing the proper food, cleaning her bowl, changing her water, doing everything he knew to make her happy. The day came for the vacation to end, and Ray prepared to pick up Sharon and her family at the airport. But as he passed the fishbowl that morning, Ray found Cleo floating belly-up. Cleo had died only 2 hours before the plane would arrive!

Ray threw his clothes on, rushed to the nearest pet store, and bought another goldfish to replace Cleo. Then he waited. He waited to see if Sharon would recognize that Cleo had been replaced by an imposter. He was afraid she would think he had failed in his responsibilities. A time of reckoning approached.

We dare not—indeed, we cannot—delete judgment

from our understanding of true Christian stewardship. Responsibility demands a reckoning. Without it, God's ownership, His sovereignty, becomes a farce. God does hold men accountable. In His parable, Jesus says that when the nobleman returned from the far country he commanded that his servants "be called unto him, to whom he had given the money, that he might know how much every man had gained by trading" (Luke 19:15). That's accountability!

Only Two Alternatives

When God tests man's stewardship, it's like a true or false test: Either it's true or it's not. The parable of the pounds illustrates this principle so clearly. The two servants who had used their master's money wisely and had multiplied it were rewarded. One was given charge over 10 cities, the other, authority over five. But the unprofitable servant was rejected. He was stripped of the one pound he did possess, and according to Matthew's account of the parable, he was cast "into outer darkness" (Matthew 25:30).

Stewardship is not to be slighted. It bears temporal as well as eternal consequences. The first step of the faithful steward is out of the world and into the household of God. That's accomplished by acknowledging Him as King, recognizing His ownership of all there is, and handing everything you have—including yourself—to Him. That must be done, or you can never be a Christian steward; you'll never be part of God's household. Without that acceptance of His lordship, you'll never be anchored. You'll drift through life, rocked to and fro by every breeze that blows. Anchor yourself in Him. Follow His principles of stewardship. Then expect abundant reward. Dare to practice Biblical economics!

2

What's on Your Mind?

Broadlawns Hospital, Des Moines, Iowa. New territory for me. I wandered down the hallways, seeking the psychiatric ward. The door locked behind me as I entered to visit an elderly man who had attempted suicide the night before. I found him and sat to talk.

The combination of drugs and alcohol had passed from Charlie's body. He seemed alert, composed, relaxed—apparently recovered. But as we talked, I was shocked as I studied the people around us. Most of them were young, but their conditions defied description. One sat near us, staring emptily at some toy blocks on a table in front of him. Another screamed uncontrollably for no apparent reason. Still another—a large, muscular, healthy-looking teenager—paced throughout the ward, shivering and shaking as if freezing to death, but with drops of sweat falling from his body. His eyes were fixed; he said nothing.

Every one of those individuals had destroyed his mind through drug abuse. After seeing them, I understood the slang expression "blow your mind." It is derived from pathetic cases just like that.

Check the Upstairs

True, not many of us fit the category of drug users

who have blown their minds. But a great many people abuse and waste their minds—not by ingesting unhealthy, addictive substances—but by absorbing, accepting, and nurturing ungodly ideas, thoughts, and attitudes. From God's point of view, that behavior is just as threatening to our spiritual welfare as drugs are to our physical and mental health.

The Christian bears the responsibility for what goes on inside his head. God calls every one of us to be good stewards of our attitudes. They deserve our most serious attention. In fact, all other aspects of our stewardship simply reflect the attitudes we harbor inside. Jesus said, "A good man out of the good treasure of the heart bringeth forth good things: and an evil man out of the evil treasure bringeth forth evil things" (Matthew 12:35). We'd better be certain we sow, water, and cultivate faithful attitudes. Scriptural economics demands careful management of the mind.

There's no question about it: The attitudes, the mindset, the thought life of the Christian, must be different from that of the non-Christian. *Transformed*, that's the only term adequate to describe it: different in nature, in character, in kind from the attitudes of the unbeliever.

The apostle Paul addressed this issue head-on when he wrote to the Christians at Ephesus: "You must no longer live as the Gentiles do, in the futility of their thinking" (Ephesians 4:17, NIV). By "Gentiles," Paul means non-Christians, those who are not among God's people. *The Living Bible* renders Paul's thought this way: "Live no longer as the unsaved do, for they are blinded and confused." Paul's point rings clear: Non-Christians' thinking and understanding are faulty; they simply cannot understand the things of God.

Sound hard to believe? Then listen to Paul's description of unbelievers in Ephesians: They have their "understanding darkened, being alienated from the life of God through the ignorance that is in them, because of the blindness of their heart" (4:18). He says the same thing in his other letters too. Listen to 1 Corinthians 2:14: "The natural man receiveth not the things of the Spirit of God: for they are foolishness unto him: neither can he know them, because they are spiritually discerned." Romans 8:5-8 also says this.

I'll never forget when I first went to work at the lumber mill in my hometown. I worked at the planer, where the finished lumber was produced. Every day I had to go to the foreman's office and pick up a work schedule that listed all the orders we were to fill during our shift. Each order began with a numeral several digits long, then there were some funny signs that looked like chicken scratches to me. After that, two or three letters appeared, maybe WF or SP or IC, then maybe something like S2S or 3T&T. And on went that list with all those crazy signs, numbers, and abbreviations.

When I first started that job, I did not understand the notations on the work schedule. But as time passed, I began to learn what all those numbers, scratches, and abbreviations meant. The initial numeral designated the order number. Those funny chicken scratches were grade marks, indicating the quality of the lumber demanded in the order. The two letters stood for the species of the wood. *WF* meant "White Fir"; *SP*, "Sugar Pine"; *IC*, "Incense Cedar." *S2S* meant "surface two sides"—in other words, make the boards smooth on two sides. *3T&T* stood for "three truck and trailer loads," the quantity of lumber needed for a specific order.

So what's the point? Simply this: Once I came to understand all those crazy signs and abbreviations, I looked at a work schedule with a new perspective. My attitude toward it was completely transformed. My understanding was no longer futile. Paul says something like that must transpire when a person moves from the realm of sin and self to the realm of salvation. His mind, his understanding, his attitudes, must be transformed. Listen to Paul's words in Ephesians 4:22-24:

> You were taught, with regard to your former way of life, to put off your old self, which is being corrupted by its deceitful desires; to be made new in the attitude of your minds; and to put on the new self, created to be like God in true righteousness and holiness (NIV).

Did you catch what verse 23 said? "Be made new in the attitude of your minds." That's the same thing Paul says to the Christians in Rome: "Be not conformed to this world: but be ye transformed by the renewing of your mind, that ye may prove what is that good, and acceptable, and perfect will of God" (Romans 12:2).

The Bible demands a transformed attitude from the Christian. It's top priority. The Christian must not maintain the same attitudes, priorities, and principles for living as the unbeliever. The stewardship of your life begins with your attitudes.

Purpose, Peace, and Position

Blessings accrue to those with transformed attitudes. Prospects for the future are bright. Scripture says those people will have purpose, peace, and position in life.

As he came to the end of his earthly journey, the apostle Paul wrote these words to his young coworker Timothy: "I know whom I have believed and am persuaded that he is able to keep that which I have committed unto him against that day" (2 Timothy 1:12).

Catch these key words in that statement: "I *know*." "I have *believed*." I "am *persuaded*." "I have *committed*."

Every one of those verbs deals with attitudes of the mind. Knowledge, belief, persuasion, commitment—they all involve man's mind, his intellect. Those attitudes of Paul's gave him purpose in life and carried him through untold difficulties. He cultivated sound attitudes toward himself, toward others, toward his work, and toward God—and that frame of mind lifted him above the filth and frustration he faced in a Roman prison as he penned his final letter. Purpose in life: Paul had it, and so can you!

The Book of Isaiah preserves these profoundly beautiful words about God: "Thou wilt keep him in perfect peace whose mind is stayed on thee: because he trusteth in thee" (26:3). The Bible promises peace to the person whose mind is fixed on God. That's an attitude of total trust, a way of thinking that looks beyond the earthly, above the physical, and focuses on the eternal. That promise of peace is much more than merely the absence of turmoil and strife. It means well-being, satisfaction, completeness—even success and prosperity (measured, of course, by God's standards, not ours). Remember this promise: "He will keep in perfect peace all those who trust in him, whose thoughts turn often to the Lord" (Isaiah 26:3, *The Living Bible*).

Scripture presents another blessing to those who manage their minds well. Paul describes it in Colossians 3:1-4:

> Since, then, you have been raised with Christ, set your hearts on things above, where Christ is seated at the right hand of God. Set your minds on things above, not on earthly things. For you died, and your life is now hidden with Christ in God. When Christ, who is your life, appears, then you also will appear with him in glory (NIV).

We have a new position in this life: "You have been raised with Christ." And we are promised a special position in the life to come: "Then you also will appear with him in glory."

But sandwiched in between those two descriptions of the Christian's position stands an urgent command: "Set your minds on things above, not on earthly things." Manage your mind! That's your responsibility as a Christian steward if you expect God's blessings to come your way.

A Constant Metamorphosis

It's true that the Bible demands different attitudes, renewed minds, for Christians, but how do you develop them? The Bible provides the answer. It sets forth sound management principles for the stewardship of your mind and attitudes.

Many large cities face a constant problem: Their downtown areas are deteriorating. Once beautiful landmarks crack, creak, and begin to crumble. Paint peels, wood rots, concrete buckles. City councils wrestle with serious decisions. Should they concern themselves with deteriorating sections of town, or simply ignore the situation and pretend it will improve on its own? Honest people know such problems won't solve themselves. A commitment to do something to correct them is what urban renewal is all about. Old structures must be refurbished or replaced. Newer buildings demand proper maintenance. It's an ongoing process that demands a continual commitment to the city to keep it in an appealing, functional condition.

That same principle applies to the care of your mind and attitudes. A continual commitment is a must; it's an ongoing process. Certainly the renewal begins when you accept Christ as your personal Saviour. That's what sets the transformation in motion. But after that, it's a lot of hard work and concerted upkeep. Paul told the Christians in Rome: "Be ye transformed by the renewing of your mind" (Romans 12:2). He was talking about a continual, ongoing process. A constant *metamorphosis*, that's precisely the word Paul used. Make a continual commitment of your mind and attitudes to Christ and to Christian standards. That's the first principle of mind management.

Make the Right Turns

The second is this: Master the options. Pretend you're strolling down a path in the park and you come to a point where it forks. Just then, you notice a sign nailed to a tree in front of you: WARNING: THE PATH LEADING NORTH IS MINED! In order to continue your journey, you have two options: Either walk to the north and risk being blown up by hidden explosives, or take the safe pathway leading south. Not much of a choice, is it? Since you know your options, you can make the right choice.

For your spiritual welfare, you must also know the options laid out before you. Some lead to destruction, others to safety. Certain attitudes and dispositions the Christian must cultivate; others he must crucify. Negative, harmful attitudes abound. Paul lists many in chapters four and five of Ephesians: deception, anger, greed, filthiness, lust, obscenity, bitterness, impurity. Some list, isn't it?

I'm sure Paul could have continued with it, but he turns to those attitudes the Christian must cultivate: honesty, kindness, compassion, forgiveness, love, thanksgiving, goodness, submission. Those are the characteristics God desires of you. Master the options! Know what God desires and seek it; know what God dislikes and shun it.

Elevate the Good

A third management principle: Meditate on the good, the right, the positive. Take a bucket of dirty, clouded water and hold it under a faucet spewing sparkling, pure water. What happens? Before long, the dirty water spills over and runs away on the ground—forced out by the pure water. The same purification can happen in your mind if you meditate on the positive.

That's why Paul told the Colossians: "Set your minds on things above, not on earthly things" (Colossians 3:2, NIV). And that's why he issued these strong words of advice to the Philippians:

> Finally, brethren, whatsoever things are true, whatsoever things are honest, whatsoever things are just, whatsoever things are pure, whatsoever things are lovely, whatsoever things are of good report; if there be any virtue, and if there be any praise, *think on these things* (4:8, emphasis mine).

As you think in your heart, so are you. That's why Jesus, especially in His Sermon on the Mount in Matthew 5 to 7, moved away from law and actions to love and attitudes. Not just the *act* of murder is wrong, but the *attitude* of anger. Not just the *act* of adultery is sinful, but the *attitude* of lust. Listen to Paul's words about unbelievers:

> They are darkened in their understanding and separated from the life of God because of the ignorance that is in them due to the hardening of their hearts. Having lost all sensitivity, they have given themselves over to sensuality so as to indulge in every kind of impurity, with a continual lust for more (Ephesians 4:18,19, NIV).

They meditate on the negative, the sinful, the filthy;

and such thoughts lead to action. That's why the Christian must meditate on the good, the right, the positive.

Company Counts

Paul pens a truth of immense importance for sound stewardship of the mind: "Do not be misled: 'Bad company corrupts good character' " (1 Corinthians 15:33, NIV). That summarizes principle number four: Move in the proper circles. Why? Because when you walk among filth, you're bound to get dirty!

What Paul says about "bad company" doesn't have to be restricted to only people. Christians must take care not to become "snooty" toward non-Christians, but neither should they be too "chummy" with them. Moving in the proper circles may mean cutting some close ties with unwholesome people. But bad company could also include the literature you read, the entertainment you attend, the fantasies you enjoy. Anything that corrupts your mind and attitudes is bad company.

Paul says, "Let all bitterness, and wrath, and anger, and clamor, and evil speaking be put away from you, with all malice" (Ephesians 4:31). Get out of the company of such evils. "Have no fellowship with the unfruitful works of darkness, but rather reprove them" (Ephesians 5:11). Don't hang around with, in, or by people, places, or things that you know full well you shouldn't. If you move in the circle of sin, it will become a noose to strangle you.

Master Model

One final principle of mind management, the most important of all: Model yourself after Jesus Christ. Paul directs his readers to be "imitators" of God (Ephesians

5:1). He admonishes the Philippian Christians to have the same attitude as that of Jesus (Philippians 2:5). Jesus must be your model in everything, including your thought life and your attitudes. That's where stewardship begins: in the mind, with the attitudes you cultivate. So many today are blowing their minds with cancerous attitudes—hatred, lust, bitterness, covetousness—attitudes that eat away at their spiritual life. Dare to be a true Christian steward. Begin by improving the management of your mind and attitudes. Then watch God's blessings accrue!

3

Go for It!

Smith Wigglesworth, the British plumber-preacher, was known as the Apostle of Faith—but not immediately. That reputation had to grow. He began by taking sick and needy people to meetings that emphasized praying for the sick.

He was so regular in bringing such people that the leaders picked him to substitute for them while they attended a convention.

"I couldn't conduct a healing service," he told them. But they persisted. It occurred to him that he didn't have to speak, all he would have to do was be in charge.

"But all whom I asked said, 'No, you have been chosen and you must do it.' And so I had to begin. I do not remember what I said but I do know that when I finished speaking fifteen people came out for healing. One of these was a man . . . who hobbled on a pair of crutches. I prayed for him and he was instantly healed. There was no one so surprised as I was."

Spiritual Gifts

Jesus didn't have time to tell His disciples everything that would happen upon the coming of His Spirit. They could not have understood Him anyway. Only the actual experience of being baptized in the Holy Spirit would enlighten their understanding.

So Jesus did not say, "After you have been filled with the Spirit you will begin to exercise spiritual gifts." The disciples would not have known what He was talking about. But as the Early Church began to minister in the Spirit's power they saw those gifts being manifested by the Spirit.

The Christians in the church at Corinth were so excited about spiritual gifts that their excitement outran their understanding. Paul had to straighten out some of their misconceptions.

But some people, even Bible scholars, have been so persuaded that such activity happened only during the Early Church period, they've used the Corinthians as an excuse not to have any manifestations of the Spirit today. That's kind of like using drunk drivers as an excuse to ban the automobile.

Such people should listen to Paul when he says, "Now concerning spiritual gifts, brethren, I would not have you *ignorant*" (1 Corinthians 12:1, emphasis mine).

Because English has borrowed the singular Greek word (*charisma*) for "spiritual gift" and given it a different meaning, we'll use the Greek plural, *charismata*, to avoid confusing the two. *Charis* is the Greek word for "grace," undeserved favor from God. *Charismata* are gifts given to us by God just because He wants to.

These supernatural gifts enable the Church to do its job. They help protect it from error, nurture its members, and reach out to the lost. Some gifts are highly visible. Others are like the rafters and floor joists in a house. Once the building is finished, they are unseen but they play a vital part in supporting and strengthening the structure.

There are two lists of spiritual gifts in Paul's writings. The main passage is 1 Corinthians 12:8-10, with two additional gifts ("helps" and "governments") mentioned in verse 28. The other passage is Romans 12:6-8, which lists some of the gifts named in the Corinthians passage but also includes additional ones. Some Bible scholars do not believe these lists are exhaustive. However, Paul most likely has written about the gifts that fill the most important roles in the Church's ministry.

Biblical Examples

Paul did not stop to explain each gift to his readers because they understood them and did not need to have them defined. The apostle simply named them.

Since Paul does not explain these gifts, where do we get such information? Gospel Publishing House has many books that define the gifts, using as a basis Biblical instances of their manifestation. The Book of Acts is the New Testament record of Church history; it is a major source of examples of spiritual gifts. However, Luke, the writer of Acts, does not stop after each incident and say, "This shows such-and-such gift at work." Even so, the examples seem rather clear. You can probably think of others.

The word of wisdom. Evident in the council meeting in Acts 15 (see verses 13-21).

The word of knowledge. Acts 10:17-20.

Faith. Not saving faith (Acts 16:31) or the fruit of faith (Galatians 5:22) but a special faith. Compare Paul's response to God's message (Acts 27:25) with Zechariah's (Luke 1:18-20).

The gifts of healing. Acts 28:8.

Miracles. Acts 20:9,10.

Prophecy. This gift sometimes involved foretelling an event (Acts 11:28; 21:10,11). However, Paul says the ministry of the prophet is for edification, exhortation, and comfort (1 Corinthians 14:3; Acts 15:32).

Discerning of spirits. The power to distinguish between the operations of the Spirit of God, evil spirits, and the unaided human spirit (1 John 4:1; 1 Timothy 4:1; 1 Corinthians 14:29).

Tongues and interpretation of tongues. A vocal means of edifying the church (1 Corinthians 14:14,15,28).

Helps. Acts 6:2,3; 1 Corinthians 16:15.

Government. The Church must have leaders. The apostles as well as men in local congregations were equipped by the Spirit to lead the Early Church. The gift of government comes through the Spirit's anointing; it is more than natural leadership qualities. Different gifts may merge in one Christian's ministry and be hardly distinguishable from each other. For example, the word of wisdom undoubtedly often operates through one who also exercises the gift of government.

Ministry. Romans 16:1,2.

Teaching. A supernatural gift that quickens the individual's understanding of the Scriptures, gives him insights he otherwise would not have, and enables him to expound the truth effectively (see Acts 13:1).

Exhortation. Romans 12:8. The exhorter is primarily a comforter, with a ministry somewhat similar to the prophet's (see Acts 14:22).

Giving. Every Christian is commanded to give. However, some appear to have a spirit of giving that goes beyond natural liberality (see Acts 11:29).

Showing mercy. Matthew 25:31-46; Acts 9:36-39.

Our Attitude Is Important

Paul says two things about spiritual gifts that might at first seem contradictory. He tells us the Holy Spirit gives these gifts "to every man severally as he will" (1 Corinthians 12:11, KJV), or "just as he chooses" (*Je-*

rusalem Bible). This stresses the sovereignty of the Spirit in determining what gifts will be manifested through individual believers. But Paul tells the Christians at Corinth to "eagerly desire spiritual gifts" (1 Corinthians 14:1).

This implies that even though the Spirit gives the gifts according to His own will, Christians should want to be used by the Spirit. Apparently our attitudes have a relationship to the operation of spiritual gifts in our lives. If we are indifferent about it we probably won't know the thrill of being used in the ministry of the gifts.

Timothy received a spiritual gift when hands were laid on him. Paul urged him not to neglect it (1 Timothy 4:14). When Paul wrote Timothy the second time he told him to "stir up" the gift (2 Timothy 1:6), like you would stir up a fire. Apparently our spiritual temperature has an influence on how much the Spirit can use us in the ministry of His gifts. We have a responsibility to keep prayed up, staying full of the Spirit and sensitive to His leading.

We will attain our highest usefulness to the Lord by recognizing that spiritual gifts are primarily for the up-building of others, not personal benefit. "As each one has received a gift, minister it to one another, as good stewards of the manifold grace of God" (1 Peter 4:10, NKJV). The life of the Church depends on this principle—each member contributing to the well-being of the others. This includes the ministry of spiritual gifts.

The "best gifts" (1 Corinthians 12:31) are those that will best meet the Church's needs in a given situation. At times, certain gifts may be needed, while other occasions may call for different gifts. We should pray earnestly that God will use us in the way that will help the greatest number of people in the congregation.

"Natural" Gifts

In addition to the Spirit's supernatural gifts, individuals have what we might term *natural* gifts. Sometimes these gifts are obviously inherited; in other instances they appear in a person whose family background does not seem to include such skills. Longtime pastor James Hamill says, "As far back as I can trace my family history, on both sides of the family, I find no preachers. Neither my forefathers nor contemporaries had much interest in the church, the Lord, or the preaching of the Word. My family did not determine or influence my vocation—God did!"[1] In whatever way we explain the presence of these abilities or talents in a person, they all come from God, the Giver of every good and perfect gift (James 1:17). They should be dedicated unreservedly to His service.

First Corinthians 4:7 emphasizes God's part in bestowing individual abilities. The principle enunciated in this verse applies to both the gifts of the Spirit and what we have been calling natural gifts: "For who makes you different from anyone else? What do you have that you did not receive? And if you did receive it, why do you boast as though you did not?" (NIV).

The number of natural gifts would be too long to attempt a list. Some individuals have unusual business ability, skill in financial matters, expertise in organization and getting people to work together, competence in office procedures. What a great contribution these people can make to their local church and to the entire work of the Kingdom. Many have manual and mechanical aptitude, building skills, designing and decorating talents. Others are artists, musicians, printers, seamstresses, cooks, writers, poets. If you have been in a church very long, you have discovered there are no abilities that cannot be put to good use.

Some may feel that because they are not carpenters, electricians, plumbers, pianists, artists, singers, or public speakers, they have nothing the Lord can use. Yet some of these people are probably unaware that their interest in others and their ability to make strangers feel at home in the church can be considered a gift from God that He wants to employ. Who knows how many have returned to church because of friendly people who smiled when they entered the door, shook their hand, and helped them find a good seat?

No one should try to copy someone else. We are individuals with our own unique personalities. God made us that way. He wants us to be ourselves and to dedicate ourselves to His glory. The task of the workers in Jesus' Parable of the Ten Pounds was to multiply their master's wealth (Luke 19:11-27). In being faithful to this responsibility, they also increased their own possessions. However, one of them did nothing with the money he was given. Consequently, he lost it! This is exactly what happens to the talents and skills we do not use. They shrivel and lose their effectiveness like muscles in our bodies that we do not exercise.

Are you willing to go for it? To give what you have to God?

Ah, but you think you haven't got much to offer. Remember Moses, how he protested being God's choice for leading His people, how inadequate he felt?

"What's that you have in your hand?" God asked.

"A staff."

"Throw it on the ground."

And it became a serpent.

God has the power. All you need is obedience, a willingness to hand whatever you have to God.

Willie Burton was a pioneer missionary to the Congo.

As he was growing up, his mother would ask him, "What's that in your hand?"

In Willie's case it was a pencil. He liked to sketch and draw. Besides making a spiritual impact on the Congo, Willie made a contribution with his natural talents: a treatise on the mind of the Luban people, knowledge of the Congo trees, paintings and drawings of the Congo, the introduction of a good breed of goats, setting up schools, clinics, maternity units.

You may have opposition. Willie did.

> Occasionally some of his friends criticized him for spending time painting. . . . After one such dose of criticism he threw his box of paints and brushes away. If this were God's will, then he would accept it without complaint. By the next mail a far better box of paints arrived . . . from a friend . . .; with tears in his eyes he acknowledged that God still wanted him to use "what was in his hand!"[2]

The Motive Counts

Now look again at 1 Peter 4:10, "Each one should use whatever gift he has received to serve others, faithfully administering God's grace in its various forms" (NIV). Peter sets forth two interrelated purposes for our gifts: The first of those purposes is for them to be used. But mere use is not enough. You may use musical talent to satisfy a desire for money. You may use tongues to draw attention to yourself. Much more crucial than mere use of any ability or gift is your motive in using it. *How* are you employing it? *Why* are you exercising it?

God grants no gifts to be used for self-gratification or self-glorification. "Each one should use whatever gift he has received *to serve others. . .*" (1 Peter 4:10, NIV, emphasis mine). Jesus said, "If anyone wants to be first, he must be the very last, and the servant of all" (Mark

9:35, NIV). Service is the keynote in Christianity. Even Jesus described His life as a time when He came not to be served but to serve and to give everything He had for the benefit of others (see Mark 10:45). That's our pattern!

It applies within the church too. When Paul discusses the matter of gifts within the church, he uses the figure of a body to convey his message. Listen:

> Just as there are many parts to our bodies, so it is with Christ's body. We are all parts of it, and it takes every one of us to make it complete, for we have different work to do. So we belong to each other, and each needs all the others (Romans 12:4,5, TLB).

What's he saying? Simply this: The church needs every individual to serve the others by employing his or her special gift from God. When that isn't happening, the church isn't functioning properly. It's sick, hurting, crippled, lame, deformed. Your brother needs your gift and you need his, not as competitor, but as colaborer.

No Self-Pity, Please

Above all, we should neither pity nor condemn ourselves because we do not possess the skills of someone else.

If we will view the Church as God does and see ourselves as members of the Body with our individual work to perform, it will help us to focus on others, not ourselves. Each time we use what God has given us, it is like a financial investment yielding compound interest. Such increase serves the dual purpose of blessing others and making us stronger and more mature. Daily put what God has given you at His disposal. Hand it to God! You'll

get back increase. Then go for it again! That's the approach to stewardship God commends.

[1]James E. Hamill, *Pastor to Pastor* (Springfield, MO: Gospel Publishing House, 1985), p. 10.

[2]Colin C. Whittaker, *Seven Pentecostal Pioneers* (Springfield, MO:
Gospel Publishing House, 1985), p. 170.

4

Watch Your Step

Remember the stories of the old West? Whatever the plot, virtually always someone was searching for gold. With pickaxes and shovels, the tired old prospectors slaved away. Then, finally, someone would spot that special chunk of metal or find a curious piece of quartz with yellowish streaks through it. Then began the shrieks of joy. The object of the hunt, the labor, and the pain had finally been found.

But the task wasn't finished yet. Before the miner would dig farther and expend any more of his energy and time, he had to take care of some very important business. Into a special pocket or pouch would go that precious rock and into town went the prospector. Once there, he headed for one of the town's most important places. No, it wasn't the bank; it wasn't the general store; it wasn't even the saloon. He went immediately to the assay office. There the old miner turned his precious possession over to a trained expert, and the assayer would carefully examine, test, and scrutinize that sample. His purpose? To test for the presence and purity of precious metals, especially gold, within that chunk of rock. Under the trained eye of the assayer, with established standards for analysis and comparison, the purity and worth of the miner's metal could be carefully and accurately determined.

Every Christian should take a lesson from the miner of old—not by hauling his or her rings, necklaces, and bracelets to the jeweler to have them appraised, but by submitting his *actions* to the same kind of meticulous test the miner insisted on for his sample. To see how pure they really are, the actions of the Christian should be checked against the standards of the Bible. The conscientious Christian is a good steward of his actions and activities.

It's Nothing New

Slogans advocating individual freedom fly high these days. We've all heard these catchy little maxims: "Do your own thing!" "I've gotta be me!" "I did it my way." "If it feels good, do it." But this mentality is nothing new. People have always sought excuses to behave however they please. That was as true in the times of the New Testament as it is today. This attitude prompted Paul to pen this exclamation in his letter to the Romans: "Shall we continue in sin, that grace may abound? God forbid. How shall we, that are dead to sin, live any longer therein?" (Romans 6:1,2).

Those words were written in response to believers in Rome who thought that if being saved by God was such a demonstration of His grace, then continuing to sin would just give further opportunity for that grace to be displayed. To Paul, whether or not they were sincere in wanting to show the world what a gracious God they served was beside the point.

That point of view has been called cheap grace. It's the attitude that degenerates into "I'm forgiven; I'll always be forgiven; so I can behave any way I please!" That's the Christian counterpart to "Do your own thing"; "If it feels good do it"; "I gotta be me"; and scores of other sin-centered slogans that try to rationalize un-biblical, non-Christian conduct.

The fact is the Christian *does* have a solemn respon-sibility to carefully guard his actions. He must assay—test, analyze, examine—them against the standards and stipulations set forth in Scripture. No economy can im-prove when principles of sound management are con-stantly violated. The Christian is called to watch his step. "Anyone who says he is a Christian should live as Christ did" (1 John 2:6, TLB). That, dear friend, is some tough assignment!

It's not hard to prove from the Bible that the Chris-tian's way of life is to be different from the non-Christian's. (See Romans 5 and 6.) Christians are called *to* certain behaviors and *from* various deeds. Everybody needs a basis for his behavior. Why should the Christian guard his step and ensure that his walk is circumspect? One of the best places to turn in the Bible for some answers is 1 Peter. Chapters one and two provide tremendous in-sight on this subject.

A Serious Injunction

Have you ever heard the term *injunction*? It's not one of our everyday terms, but it crops up every now and then in the news in a legal context. An injunction is a judicial order requiring someone to do or refrain from doing some specified action. An injunction demands something specific. It says, "You may do this, but not that." Or, "You must stop doing this, and you must start doing that." An injunction requires conformity to its stip-ulations, or more serious steps of correction will be taken.

An injunction is precisely what God places on His people. Peter simply relays the words of God: "Be ye holy; for I am holy" (1 Peter 1:16). In fact, Peter merely repeats what God has always required of His people. That statement is a direct quotation by Peter from the Old Testament Book of Leviticus (11:44,45). Holiness is nothing new; God has always demanded it from His people. The call for holiness rings forth from Leviticus four times. The word *holy* pops up so often in Leviticus that holiness becomes the theme of the book. That's right! Leviticus is a guidebook to holiness. God is saying to Israel in Leviticus: "If you plan to be My people, then here's what you'd better do, and here's what you'd better not do!" God has always established a high standard of behavior for His people, and then demanded a high level of obedience to that standard.

Of course, some of the specifics of the actions of God's people have changed since Christ's work on Calvary, but the principles haven't. For example, the command to be holy booms forth from Leviticus 19:2. Then follows a whole list of specifics concerning how to carry out that injunction: Respect your father and mother. Observe the Lord's Day. Don't practice idolatry in any form. And the list goes on. God says, "Consecrate yourselves and be holy, because I am the Lord your God. Keep my decrees and follow them. I am the Lord, who makes you holy" (Leviticus 20:7,8, NIV).

Notice the words in those verses: *keep, follow, consecrate.* Those are *action* words. "Make certain your actions are in keeping with My guidelines!" That's God's concern in Leviticus—and that's still God's concern for His people. When Peter cited that statement from Leviticus—"Be holy, because I am holy"—he, along with his readers, knew full well all that went along with it. Certain standards of conduct are expected of God's people. This injunction must be firmly fixed in your mind and heart as an unbending principle of sound scriptural stewardship.

What's in It for Me?

Not long ago, a prince in the royal line of a prominent nation became involved in an unseemly relationship with a young woman. Publicity ran rampant concerning the incident; newspapers, radio stations, and television newscasts simply couldn't ignore it. If anyone else, any of us "common folk," had been involved in that same situation, no one would have paid much attention. But a *prince*—now that's a different matter! Here was a man with royal blood, a man with a rich heritage, a man with a kingdom as an inheritance. Such conduct was hardly becoming a member of the royal household!

Listen to these words of Peter about Christians: "You are a chosen people, a royal priesthood, a holy nation, a people belonging to God" (1 Peter 2:9, NIV). Christians are part of a royal line. And that regal heritage demands a demeanor becoming to our position. God has chosen us; we are His; we're a royal priesthood, a holy nation.

All of those designations have at least one thing in common: They all describe a people much different from the multitudes in our world. And that's what the word *holy* is all about. Basically, it means "to be set apart," to be separated for a specific purpose. To be holy is to be different. Not peculiar, in the sense of being weird, but different from the masses because the Christian's attitudes, priorities, and actions are different.

The Christian has an inheritance, and because he is an heir to the blessings of the kingdom of God, his conduct must testify to that royal lineage. Note carefully these words of Paul:

> Now the works of the flesh are manifest, which are these, adultery, fornication, uncleanness, lasciviousness, idolatry, witchcraft, hatred, variance, emulations, wrath, strife, se-

ditions, heresies, envyings, murders, drunkenness, revel-
ings, and such like: of the which I tell you before, as I have
also told you in time past, that they which do such things
shall not inherit the kingdom of God (Galatians 5:19-21).

You can't say it more plainly: Christians must maintain
conduct befitting the King if they desire His royal inheritance.

What's the Point?

Have you ever watched a professional figure skater?
I'll never forget watching a famous husband-wife figure
skating team from Russia during a practice session. They
seemed to skate so easily, so freely, so gracefully. But
every move was carefully timed, every jump perfectly
executed, every spin meticulously critiqued. They knew
that when they skated in competition they would be
judged, and the slightest flaw, the smallest mistake, would
drag down their score. They had to make certain that
not one move was wrong, that everything contributed
to the highest possible score from the judges.

Just like the moves of those skaters, every action of
the Christian deserves careful scrutiny. Peter says that
Christians are people with a purpose in life. What is that
purpose? To "show forth the praises of him who hath
called you out of darkness into his marvelous light"
(1 Peter 2:9).

Jesus says it too, in His Sermon on the Mount: "Let
your light so shine before men, that they may see your
good works, and glorify your Father which is in heaven"
(Matthew 5:16). Did you catch that last part? "That they
may see your good *works* and glorify your Father which
is in heaven." The purpose of the Christian is to bring
praise and glory to God by his life, including the way he
acts. Look again at those verses from Galatians 5 and

compare them with what Paul says in Ephesians 4:29 to 5:7. It's pretty hard to deny, isn't it? God expects proper behavior from His people.

Probably the best summary appears in Ephesians 5:15: "Be careful how you act" (TLB). You've got to be careful because the way you act should bring praise and glory to God. A good steward makes his master look good. How do you measure up?

Beware of Watching Eyes

"A man never sees the worst in himself until it appears in his children." That old saying emphasizes the importance of one person's influence on another. Have you ever considered the tremendous influence people have on you? Just stop and think for a minute about all the people you encounter on a regular basis. Do you look up to some of them? Do some have characteristics or dispositions or habits or jobs or families you especially like? Can you think of people who have influenced your thinking or behavior, no matter how slight?

You can probably think of several people who affect your life in some way. But consider this: You influence people, too. It starts early. The child influences the toddler. The teen influences the child. The collegian influences the teen. You have had and will continue to have an influence on others. Sons become like their fathers. Daughters become like their mothers. Athletes reflect their coaches, students their teachers. Why do you think fashions follow the trends set by the superstars? People influence people!

And think about this: Christians have a tremendous influence on non-Christians. I know it doesn't always seem like it, but it's true. That's what Jesus was talking about when He said His followers should let their lights shine, then other people will see how they behave—they'll see their deeds—and glorify God.

Listen to the way Peter puts it: "Live such good lives among the pagans that, though they accuse you of doing wrong, they may see your good deeds and glorify God on the day he visits us" (1 Peter 2:12, NIV). Make your influence count for good. It's trite, but true, the only gospel some people will ever read is the gospel written by your life. Make it count, as a profitable steward in God's kingdom. Push others toward God with your holy influence.

But What If . . .

Not everyone walks circumspectly through this life. Some people have serious problems in their attempts to maintain holy behavior. What if you're having problems with your actions? What should you do if you know that you are failing to carry out God's call to a life of purity? What must you do if you are not functioning as a good steward of your actions? Try these simple steps:

1. Recognize you're wrong. Admit it; face up to it. The Bible is very clear about what God expects. Don't try to push sinful behavior under the rug. It will end up destroying the whole fabric of your life. Get it out in the open where you can deal with it.

2. Repent. That's an old-fashioned word and an old-fashioned idea, but it's still very important in God's economy. It means to be sorry for what you've been doing and to purpose in your heart to stop, turn around, and go in the opposite direction.

3. Let go of that wrong behavior. You've got to hand it to God. Confess it to Him, then accept His forgiveness. Understand that He won't hold those past mistakes against you.

4. Rely on the Lord for help and deliverance. Don't expect to overcome your problems on your own. You've got to rely regularly on His help. As you pray, read the Bible, and fellowship with other Christians, the power of the Holy Spirit can lead you to victory over any sinful behavior that dogs your path.

Practice Biblical management principles in dealing with your actions, and then watch your spiritual economy improve.

5

Those Fleeting Moments

Our younger son had ear problems. We had to seek medical attention from a specialist whose office was over 2 hours away. On two different occasions we made the trip, arrived in ample time for our appointment, and sat patiently, expecting to be summoned into the doctor's examining room very shortly.

The waiting room was full of people and cluttered with magazines, toys, and overflowing ashtrays. The noise increased, it seemed, with every minute we waited. On both visits we finally entered the doctor's presence nearly an hour after our designated appointment, only to be hurried in and out in 5 to 10 minutes, each time receiving less than desirable treatment both medically and personally.

Following the second visit, we decided it was unnecessary to continue our relationship with that physician. The doctor's demeanor was unsatisfactory; his attitude wanting. But the most frustrating thing was his lack of availability. Extended stays in his waiting room, coupled with rushed treatments in his examining room, convinced us that *his* time was valuable—but *ours* wasn't! He needed to reevaluate his use of patients' time to ensure that their time wasn't wasted. He badly needed to adjust his availability. And because he didn't, he lost at least one opportunity to serve.

Some Christians need to do the same thing: to reevaluate, to reconsider, and to readjust the manner in which they use their time. If the Christian envisions a scriptural economy for his life, he must manage his time wisely and well. The good steward is the Christian whose availability to the Lord and the Lord's work is properly understood and in proper adjustment. That availability centers in many ways on how that person uses his or her time.

How Sweet It Is

When the apostle Paul writes to the Christians in Ephesus, he zeros in on the matter of time in just a few short verses in chapter 5. He presents some important principles pertinent to Christians of every age.

"See then that ye walk circumspectly, not as fools, but as wise" (Ephesians 5:15). In other words, Paul is encouraging the Ephesians to be very careful how they live. He might just as well have said, "Watch how you spend your time!" How easy it is to forget that time is a precious possession; it's so fleeting. Time demands great care because it's a very precious commodity.

Why do we consider time so precious? Because we have only so much. God is the creator and controller of time. That's one of the greatest lessons we can learn from the opening chapters of the Bible. The Book of Genesis reveals to us that when God spoke, time was created along with everything else. The act of creation—when God spoke the universe into existence—began the ticking of time. The only one who can make time stand still is the same one who set it in motion. God is the controller of time; we aren't. Our time is allotted by Him; each of us is granted a portion of time at His discretion. That makes it very precious.

You've witnessed this school scene before; maybe

you've even participated in it: The bell rings announcing the conclusion of class and the beginning of a 5-minute break between periods. Out from the classroom rushes an eager young man, down the hallway, to a special place, where he meets that special girl. There they stand, perhaps saying very little, but they're together and that's what matters.

The seconds tick into minutes, urging them to hurry to their next class before the bell rings, but they wait as long as possible. Then, suddenly, the fellow leaves the girl at the door of her classroom and rushes toward his next class. Just in the nick of time he slides into his desk in unison with the clanging of the bell. Why would anyone behave like that? For two simple reasons: Every moment he has with the object of his affection is precious, and he has such a limited amount.

Every Christian should consider his time just as precious. Time deserves your utmost care and attention. It deserves the controlling influence of spiritual wisdom. "See then that ye walk circumspectly, not as fools, but as wise" (Ephesians 5:15).

Recognize that your time is precious. Take time to read some other passages from the Bible that support this thought. Look at Psalm 90:10-12; Ecclesiastes 3:1-8 and 12:1-8; Hebrews 9:27. Remember, the time you waste can never be reclaimed. You may be forgiven for squandering time, but you can never be granted the opportunity to reuse it. Once it's gone, time is forever lost.

Listen to these words from James:

> Now listen, you who say, "Today or tomorrow we will go to this or that city, spend a year there, carry on business and make money." Why, you do not even know what will happen tomorrow. What is your life? You are a mist that appears for a little while and then vanishes. Instead, you ought to say, "If it is the Lord's will, we will live and do

this or that." As it is, you boast and brag. All such boasting is evil. Anyone, then, who knows the good he ought to do and doesn't do it, sins (James 4:13-17, NIV).

Anyone who knows the value of time and squanders it sins! Realize how precious your time is—and treat it accordingly.

That's Heavy!

Good stewardship of your time demands a second serious recognition: Great pressure weighs on your time. Listen again to Paul's words: "Be very careful, then, how you live—not as unwise but as wise, making the most of every opportunity, because the days are evil" (Ephesians 5:15,16, NIV). Mark those last words well: "because the days are evil." The days in which we live *are* evil, and because of that, there is tremendous pressure on the Christian to misuse time.

Paul writes pointedly of the pressures that push God's people. His words accurately describe our own day:

> In the last days perilous times shall come. For men shall be lovers of their own selves, covetous, boasters, proud, blasphemers, disobedient to parents, unthankful, unholy, without natural affection, trucebreakers, false accusers, incontinent, fierce despisers of those that are good, traitors, heady, high-minded, lovers of pleasures more than lovers of God; having a form of godliness, but denying the power thereof: from such turn away (2 Timothy 3:1-5).

In 2 Timothy 2:16 Paul advises against wasting time in "godless chatter." And in verse 23 he urges Timothy to have nothing to do with stupid and foolish arguments. Paul admonishes the Thessalonian Christians to stay away from those who are idle and do not live according to sound Christian principles (2 Thessalonians 3:6). And if

you think that you would never be guilty of such behavior, don't consider yourself home free. In this our
land of opportunity, many pursuits don't obviously fall
under the category "Unacceptable for Christians." Rather,
they are a matter of priorities, what God would have us
give our time to—since we have this fixed amount.

People who are failing miserably in the stewardship
of their time fill the pews of churches on Sunday. How
about you? How wisely are you managing the moments
of each day, the months of each year? Maybe the pressure
has gotten to you. Maybe you've given in to the temp-
tations and the forces that surround you. The Christian
who squanders and mismanages money is rebuked and
reprimanded. And so should be the Christian who squanders and mismanages time.

Now, step back a minute, and let's take time to clarify
a potential problem. The Bible does not say you should
constantly be hurrying and scurrying here and there,
forever raising clouds of dust in your service for the Lord.
Good stewardship of time does not equal constant busy-
ness with "the Lord's work." Proper time management
includes periods of leisure—times to relax, to rest, to be
renewed; times of recreation and re-creation. Jesus with-
drew on occasion to be alone, to pray, to rest; and He
encouraged His disciples to do likewise (Mark 6:31,32).
Constant activity is not the key to scriptural stewardship
of time.

The crux of the matter is this: Have you brought *all*
of your time under the lordship of Jesus Christ? That
was the problem with the businessmen in the Book of
James. Take a quick mental inventory of the manner in
which you spend your time. What do you find? How
satisfied are you with your stewardship of time?

The average American adult spends about 4½ hours
a day watching television. Now television is a marvelous

invention, and it carries great potential for good. But when God's people watch it indiscriminately and allow it to eat up their time, it becomes a dangerous enemy.

Television is only one example of many that draw Christians into wasting valuable time. The drugs that infest society, the trash that litters newsstands, the craze that surrounds athletics—all of these tempt Christians to squander time.

The days *are* evil. As Christians we must recognize the pressures and refuse to relinquish our right to the time God has given us.

Grab All You Can Get!

Imagine yourself in a contest and you've just won the grand prize: a 2-minute shopping spree at your local supermarket. The bell sounds, and you're on your way up and down the aisles, grabbing, scooping, and shoveling as much merchandise into your basket as fast as you can. You know the time is limited, so you've got to make the most of it.

The buzzer sounds; your time's up. Whatever you've piled into your basket is all you get. But you did your best. You worked rapidly and accomplished as much as you could in the time you had. Now you must be satisfied with your effort.

Paul says Christians need to have that same sort of mind-set. In Ephesians 5:16 he instructs his readers to redeem the time. Or, as a number of other versions render it: Make the most of every opportunity that comes your way!

That doesn't mean you constantly scurry around, as if you were a bundle of endless energy. It doesn't even mean you sit down and divide up your time and say: "Let's see, this week I'll give 40 hours to my job, 15 to my family, 10 to my social life, 10 to myself, and 5 to the Lord's work. That leaves 88 hours for eating, sleeping, and all the other necessities of life."

No, it doesn't mean that at all. Rather, it means you view every moment of your life as a precious gift to be used to the full. Your time is a sacred trust granted you by God. Your responsibility is to seize every opportunity and make it count for the good. Walk down the aisles of life savoring the opportunities and the blessings that befall you.

That's God's will for every one of us. Paul instructs us: "Be ye not unwise, but understanding what the will of the Lord is" (Ephesians 5:17). The Lord's will is that you might "do good" by being constantly filled with the Spirit (Ephesians 5:18). The stewardship of your time must involve time for personal spiritual growth. That's doing good for yourself. You can do good for others by speaking words of encouragement through psalms, hymns, and spiritual songs (Ephesians 5:19). You can redeem your time and carry out God's will by giving thanks to God the Father for everything (Ephesians 5:20).

That's what stewardship of time is all about. It's seizing opportunities, savoring blessings, serving others. It means trusting God's guidance and then doing your best wherever and whenever opportunities arise. You may use your time to brood over losses, to reopen old wounds, to feed bitter grudges, to weep over bygone opportunities—but that's wasting, not redeeming, your time. To waste your time is to fail as a Christian steward. Instead, recognize that God has a purpose for your time and strive to redeem every opportunity.

A Turn Here, A Twist There

I once had a car that tried my patience. The engine

timing regularly went out of whack, causing the engine to sound like cymbals clanging under the hood. I'd pull over to the side of the road, lift the hood, take out a few tools, loosen a bolt, make a quick adjustment, hop back in, and head down the road. Sometimes it took two or three tries to get the adjustment right. But just that little turn here and twist there made the car run better.

Sometimes Christians need to stop and make a few adjustments in their priorities. They need to adjust their availability so they are better prepared to redeem the time God has granted them. Everyone receives a different portion of time, just as everyone receives a different portion of wealth and abilities. It's not a matter of how long you serve, but how faithfully.

Be assured that faithfulness in the stewardship of your time pays great dividends. In fact, Scripture indicates that God prepares rewards for those who have redeemed their time through faithful service. That message rings clear in Paul's final letter, a letter he wrote on the verge of his execution at the hands of the Roman government. Listen to the confidence of these verses:

> I am now ready to be offered, and the time of my departure is at hand. I have fought a good fight, I have finished my course, I have kept the faith: henceforth there is laid up for me a crown of righteousness, which the Lord, the righteous judge, shall give me at that day: and not to me only, but unto them also that love his appearing (2 Timothy 4:6-8).

Time is a sacred trust. Manage it carefully and anticipate rewards; squander it, and expect judgment.

6

Test Those Tastes

An old Englishman acquired a magical monkey's paw. Three wishes were his for the asking. Immediately he wished for a pile of money. In a short while, a messenger arrived at the Englishman's door and announced that the old man's son had been fatally injured in an auto accident. When insurance claims were settled, the Englishman received his pile of money, but its arrival was marred because it cost him his son.

So the old man grasped the magical paw and voiced his second wish: that his son might live again. That meant forfeiting his newfound fortune, but his desire for his son overwhelmed his desire for money. Suddenly, he heard a slow, arduous clomping sound approaching. In anticipation, he flung open the door, only to look in disbelief on his crippled, scarred son. The old Englishman reasoned that life in such condition was worse than death, so he used up the power of the magical paw to fulfill his third desire: that his son might be dead again!

That tale illustrates an important truth: People seldom give careful consideration to the nature, the cost, and the consequences of the desires that motivate their thoughts and actions. Everyone has desires, longings, wants—and there's nothing wrong with that. But the Bible says the Christian must hand his desires to God. He must test his tastes, weigh his desires, and examine the wants and wishes that compete for control in his life. Biblical stewardship demands attention to every aspect of life; it's a total "economic" system.

Why do you do what you do during a normal day? What desires drive you? The New Testament teaches that we can choose to be ruled by the lust of the flesh, the lust of the eyes, the pride of life, or the will of God (see 1 John 2:16,17). For each option, the Bible provides examples of individuals who selected that pathway. While you read the rest of this chapter, compare your desires with those of the Biblical characters. Examine your longings, especially those that direct your decisions. Determine where you stand as a steward of your desires. What desires drive you?

Demas the Worldling

Ever heard of Demas? He's mentioned three times in the New Testament. He was a companion and coworker of the apostle Paul. In Philemon 24, Paul lists Demas among those who send greetings to Philemon, Apphia, Archippus, and their congregation. And that was quite a group! It included Epaphras, the man who first preached the gospel in Colossae and pioneered the church there. It included the Gospel writer Mark, who was also Paul and Peter's coworker, and a cousin of Barnabas. It included Luke, the faithful physician and traveling companion of Paul, who wrote the Gospel of Luke and the Book of Acts. No question about it, Demas was right there with the "big boys"!

That's true when Paul mentions Demas in Colossians 4:14, too. He's a colaborer with Paul, who is in prison and badly in need of support. But something sounds fishy here. Paul brings Colossians to a close as he names those with him as helpers: Aristarchus, Mark, Jesus Justus,

Epaphras, Luke, and Demas. Every one of those men receives a word of commendation—except Demas. Could there be a problem? Is something wrong? Is Demas failing in his commitment, in his desire to serve?

The sad truth jumps from 2 Timothy 4:10. The apostle Paul, once again in prison and needing support, pens a short, poignant postscript about Demas: "Demas hath forsaken me, having loved this present world, and is departed unto Thessalonica." Others had left Paul too. Crescens went to Galatia; Titus to Dalmatia; Tychicus to Ephesus. But they went as servants of God and of Paul. Demas went to Thessalonica, not as a servant of God, but as a servant of self and the world.

Demas desired the world, "this present world," said Paul, the world that passes away, said John (1 John 2:17). He rubbed shoulders with spiritual giants of the Early Church without much appreciation for it. His desires were bounded by his five senses. His horizons were limited to where the earth met the sky. Certainly he didn't see the city "whose builder and maker is God" (Hebrews 11:10). That takes faith—and a taste for eternity.

Demas is a sobering example to us. As Christians we must remember our responsibility as stewards under God and guard against the temptation to become like Demas.

Demetrius the Godmaker

Two men in the New Testament bear the name Demetrius, but Acts 19 records a story about the Demetrius we're interested in. He wasn't a Christian, but rather a craftsman in the city of Ephesus, where the great temple of the Greek goddess Artemis stood. The worship of Artemis thrived in ancient Ephesus.

Paul arrived in Ephesus to engage in a vigorous ministry of preaching and teaching. For more than 2 years he ministered, and God blessed the work with marvelous results. Take a quick look at the first part of Acts 19 and read for yourself what happened. The Spirit fell, miracles occurred, victories came repeatedly. But the blessings of God wrought havoc with other established practices in Ephesus.

Demetrius called a summit meeting of Ephesian businessmen. The revival in Ephesus severely cut into the profits Demetrius derived from making silver statues of Artemis.

" 'Men,' " Demetrius proclaimed, " 'you know we receive a good income from this business. And you see and hear how this fellow Paul has convinced and led astray large numbers of people here in Ephesus and in practically the whole province of Asia. He says that manmade gods are no gods at all. There is danger not only that our trade will lose its good name, but also that the temple of the great goddess Artemis will be discredited, and the goddess herself, who is worshipped thoughout the province of Asia and the world, will be robbed of her divine majesty' " (Acts 19:25-27, NIV).

Demetrius' words worked. A riot broke out, fueled by the chant, "Great is Artemis of the Ephesians!" Soon the entire city reeled. Paul's coworkers, Gaius and Aristarchus, were dragged into the theater to face a mob of angry rioters.

What a mess! But what's so pathetic about the situation is the comment in verse 32: "The assembly was in confusion: Some were shouting one thing, some another. Most of the people did not even know why they were there" (NIV). But Demetrius knew exactly why he was there. He tried to cover his real motive by faking a concern for the goddess and her temple. But his true motivation became obvious when he proclaimed to his fellow citizens, in effect: "You know we make good money from this statue-making business. We can't let some outsider come in here and ruin it for us!"

His problem wasn't really a concern for Artemis or her temple or even a disagreement with Paul and what he was saying. His concern was economics. Demetrius desired dollars! Everything else paled in comparison to maintaining that "good income." Nothing could compete with that hunger for money and material prosperity.

Does that strike a sensitive spot in you? Beware the power of finances in your life. Nowhere does the Bible lift up poverty as the Christian ideal, but neither does it recommend making wealth a goal. The kingdom of God is the Christian's goal, and affection for money is a stumbling block along the way: "Some people, eager for money, have wandered from the faith and pierced themselves with many griefs" (1 Timothy 6:10, NIV). Establish sound attitudes toward money right now, and purpose never to compromise your scriptural principles for the sake of material gain. Learn from the negative example of Demetrius.

Diotrephes the First

Tucked away toward the back of the Bible is a little letter called 3 John. The apostle John wrote that Epistle as a personal message to a man named Gaius. The issue John addressed is the reception of traveling preachers by Christian congregations. Gaius excelled in his openness and hospitality toward them, but in the same congregation was a man named Diotrephes. Listen to what John wrote about him:

> I wrote to the church, but Diotrephes, who loves to be first, will have nothing to do with us. So if I come, I will

call attention to what he is doing, gossiping maliciously about us. Not satisfied with that, he refuses to welcome the brothers. He also stops those who want to do so and puts them out of the church (3 John 9,10, NIV).

The problem festering in Diotrephes' life jumps out from verse 9: He loved to be first. Diotrephes desired distinction. He refused to submit to some old apostle named John. He wasn't about to let some evangelist come into his congregation and steal his glory—and he wasn't about to let anybody else in the congregation welcome the traveling preacher either. That might mean loss of influence, a lessening of his power. Diotrephes desired distinction, and nothing could stand in his way!

How do you spell *sin*? For Diotrephes, sin has to be spelled *s-I-n*. The big *I* is the problem. Self-importance, personal preeminence, status, power, prestige—at the expense of others and the progress of God's work—that was Diotrephes' sin.

Have you ever been around someone who always had to be the center of attention, to be in charge, to dominate others? That kind of person is a modern-day Diotrephes, a person who "loves to be first." People like that usually aren't pleasant to be around; their attitudes and behavior contradict Christian principles.

The Bible clearly says that in all things Christ must have the preeminence (Colossians 1:18). And Christians are called to humility, to a servant mind-set (Matthew 5:3; 18:1-5; 20:25-28), not to arrogance and unhealthy self-exaltation.

In our world of overinflated egos, how rampant runs the desire of Diotrephes! Guard yourself; watch your motives. Root out any tendencies toward the sin of Diotrephes. The management principles governing your life must exclude those unhealthy urges for personal prestige and power. The good steward lets God take care of the promotions. After all, He's the real manager under whom the Christian serves.

Dorcas the Disciple

Three men with three different problems, that's what we've seen so far. But then there's Dorcas, a gracious Christian renowned for her charity in the church at Joppa. Luke paints a beautiful picture of this little-known lady. Acts 9 says Dorcas constantly did her best to meet the needs of the poor. She sewed robes and other articles of clothing, and distributed them to those in need. Her works brought her praise, especially from the widows in Joppa.

Listen to Luke's evaluation of Dorcas: "There was a woman in Joppa, a disciple called Tabitha, whose name in Greek was Dorcas (meaning Gazelle). She was a woman whose whole life was full of good and kindly actions" (Acts 9:36, Phillips).

Dorcas is the only woman specifically called a disciple in the New Testament. Let us take a close look at this woman having such a distinction. Discipleship was her heartbeat; to be and do what God desired. Nothing more, nothing less. Her devotion, her dedication, her deeds of kindness, grew out of her determination to be the best disciple of the Lord Jesus Christ she could, driven—not by a desire for worldly pleasures or money or power—but by a hunger to be as much like Jesus as possible. He went about doing good; so would she.

The desires of a Christian are important. God expects good stewardship in this area just as much as in any other area. He expects sound, scriptural management. How often do *your* wants and wishes interfere with *God's* directions for your life?

What God desires and expects of you may *not* always coincide with your desires. Jesus himself taught us this when He prayed in the Garden of Gethsemane just before His arrest and crucifixion. Remember? More than once He prayed to the Father, "Not my will, but thine be done." He wanted the Father to take the cup of suffering away. Jesus had no desire to suffer; His *personal* desire was for God to find some other way for man's sin problem to be remedied. But He submitted His own desire to the will of the Father. That's the example we must follow. You've gotta hand your desires to God!

The Unholy Trinity

All that is in the world, the lust of the flesh, and the lust of the eyes, and the pride of life, is not of the Father, but is of the world. And the world passeth away, and the lust thereof; but he that doeth the will of God abideth for ever (1 John 2:16,17).

Those three things in verse 16—the lust of the flesh, the lust of the eyes, and the pride of life—form an "unholy trinity." Christians serious about their stewardship need to beware of them. These words of John indict Demas, Demetrius, and Diotrephes: Demas went after the lust of the flesh, the sensual satisfaction of the world. Demetrius couldn't control the lust of his eyes; he had to have what money could buy. Diotrephes was full of pride and arrogance. All three stand convicted by the words of John.

Dorcas, on the other hand, easily represents the one who does the will of God. John says that person will live forever. Thus it seems—on a symbolic level—quite fitting that after Dorcas had fallen ill and died, Peter prayed for her and God restored her to life. (Read it for yourself in Acts 9.)

59

Life awaits those who carry out not their own will but the desire of God. That's God's promise. Shun the desires of Demas, Demetrius, and Diotrephes, and strive for a life of discipleship. Check your desires, those longings that motivate you. Where are you headed? Set your standards by Scripture and serve as a faithful steward of your desires.

7

Ready for a Real Relationship?

Legend says Daniel Boone and his wife were standing outside their wilderness home one day when a family of new settlers rode by. Boone inquired about their destination. "Oh, about 60 or 70 miles up ahead," came the reply. When the conversation ended and the travelers left, Boone turned to his wife. "It's time for us to move on," he said. "They're beginning to close in on us."

Have you ever felt like movin' on because people seemed to be closing in on you? These days most of us don't have a lot of room. The wide-open spaces are shrinking incredibly fast, and that puts a responsibility on every one of us. We all have to relate to people around us. Relationships form a tremendously important part of life. In fact, Christians, of all people, need to nurture some very important relationships. It's part of stewardship. How well we manage our relationships is a measure of the health of our spiritual economy.

Me, Myself, and I

Amnesia. You know what that is. It's when a person can't remember anything. No name, no home, no family, no job—everything vanishes from memory. The person is mentally stranded, not knowing who he is, where he came from, or where he's going. That's a pitiful condition.

Good stewards must guard against spiritual amnesia. Every Christian must be properly related to himself, knowing who he is, where he came from, and where he's going. Paul speaks to that in Colossians 3. His thrust is this: You are a Christian; *therefore* you have new obligations and new responsibilities toward yourself. You've got to relate to yourself in a different manner than you did before. That's part of Christian stewardship.

The crux of what Paul says in Colossians 3:5-11 is this twofold directive: Off with the old, on with the new!

I don't know about you, but I hate trying on new clothes. The prospect of new clothes is great, but I dislike going into one of those little cubicles in a clothing store and taking off my old clothes. But it has to be done before I can put on the new ones.

Spiritually, we have to do the same thing. "Put to death," Paul says, "whatever belongs to your earthly nature" (Colossians 3:5, NIV). Take it off, just like an old, filthy garment.

There will always be people who say that's not necessary. You don't need to clean up your act. They were saying that in ancient Colossae, too. But that's not Scripture. Clean out the closets; destroy those old, outdated, sin-soiled garments. Crucify anger, wrath, malice, slander, lust, greed; they're not in style for the Christian.

Replace them with the classic in Christian fashion: "Put on the new man, which is renewed in knowledge after the image of him that created him" (Colossians 3:10). Good stewardship requires crucifying the sinful and cultivating the sacred. The new garment leaves no room for those old habits that fracture relationships and give birth to bitterness. Put on the new garment, and you'll find old prejudices destroyed. Paul says so in Colossians 3:11. Put it on, and you'll find that Jesus becomes more and more important to you.

I remember back when guys loved faded jeans. The older, more faded they got, the better. They improved every time they were put on. That's what the Christian's new garment is like. It just gets better and better the longer it's worn. Make sure you wear the clothing of Christianity. Consistently. Then follow through on Paul's injunction in Colossians 4:2 (NIV): "Devote yourselves to prayer, being watchful and thankful."

Bind Us Together

I'll never forget being drafted onto my first little league baseball team. I was only 8, but I was in there with the big boys, those 11- and 12-year-olds. What a privilege; how proud I was to be a part of that team. Along with everybody else, I did my best every time I played.

As a Christian, you've been drafted onto God's team, the Church. That's a privilege, but you've got to relate to the other team members. The best way to do that is by recognizing your common privileges and your common responsibilities. Every Christian assumes a new uniform when he enters the Church. We've talked about that already. But listen to Paul's description of that uniform:

> As God's chosen people, holy and dearly loved, clothe yourselves with compassion, kindness, humility, gentleness and patience. Bear with each other and forgive whatever grievances you may have against one another. Forgive as the Lord forgave you. And over all these virtues put on love, which binds them all together in perfect unity (Colossians 3:12-14, NIV).

Several other things are essential to the welfare of both you and your church. Colossians 3:15 says Christians have a new umpire. You know what an umpire is. He's the official in a baseball game who gets bad-mouthed by the fans: "Kill the umpire!" But everybody knows the umpire is indispensable to the order and outcome of the game. Paul sees the possibility of strife arising even within the church, so he says, "Let the peace . . . from . . . Christ rule (act as umpire continually) in your hearts" (Colossians 3:15, *The Amplified Bible*). A new umpire! The peace of Christ should pronounce the verdict whenever differences threaten to disturb the unity of the fellowship. When love and bitterness contend for mastery, peace must be the governing principle.

Besides getting a new uniform and a new umpire, when a person becomes a Christian he has a new rulebook. I've been in schools where well-thought-out rules produced an atmosphere in which learning could effectively occur. Paul says the church has a "rulebook" to keep it pure, orderly, informed. In fact, Paul's imagery in verse 16 is of the rulebook as a housekeeper. He says we should "let the word of Christ [the Bible] dwell in us, or *keep house*, not as a servant but as a master" (*Matthew Henry's Commentary*). It should have control; it should direct activity, as the manager of the house. The word of Christ will even clean the dirty corners, if Christians allow it to dwell richly within and among them.

A Leader and an Obligation

Team leaders are irreplaceable in sports. They encourage, inspire, instruct, and unite the players. The Church also has a team leader. "Whatsoever ye do," Paul writes, "in word or deed, do all in the name of the Lord Jesus" (Colossians 3:17). Look to Him as leader, example, inspirer. Let His leadership become a uniting force that joins you in a positive relationship with the rest of the Church.

Then accept a serious obligation, summed up in one word: *intercession*. The new responsibility placed on the shoulders of every Christian is to pray for others. Listen to Paul's plea:

> Devote yourselves to prayer, being watchful and thankful. And pray for us, too, that God may open a door for our message, so that we may proclaim the mystery of Christ, for which I am in chains. Pray that I may proclaim it clearly, as I should (Colossians 4:2-4, NIV).

Intercessory prayer—intervening prayer on behalf of others—is the Christian's responsibility. Exodus 17:8-13 gives a beautiful example of intercessory prayer: holding up the hands of another in time of need and weakness. Look at Acts 12:1-17 and marvel at the way intercessory prayer can break chains of bondage. It's the Christian's greatest weapon. Exercise it. Then watch your spiritual condition and the spiritual climate of your church prosper.

A new uniform, a new umpire, a new rulebook, a new team leader, a new obligation—you need them all to maintain fruitful relationships within your local church. Be a wise steward of the privileged position you enjoy. Cultivate relationships within the church.

Another Family

Besides your church family, you're most likely part of another family, a smaller one. Everybody fits into the category of a father or mother, son or daughter, husband or wife. Even though you didn't have a choice about some of these relationships, you're part of a family, and relationships within the family are among the most important and precious on earth.

The apostle Paul speaks to this issue, too. Apparently,

it was a matter of concern even in his day, and who today would dare say it's not a constant concern in our world! Take a few minutes to read Ephesians 5:21 to 6:4. Then read 1 Peter 3:1-7 to get Peter's ideas. Relationships within the family are crucial. The Christian's call urges him to make family relationships top priority. How well you care for your relationships at home is a measure of your stewardship.

Husbands, fathers, wives, children—Paul speaks to all. "Husbands, love your wives and be not bitter against them. . . . Fathers, provoke not your children to anger, lest they be discouraged" (Colossians 3:19,21). For the wives, Paul advises Christian submission (Colossians 3:18). (Notice: Nowhere does he direct husbands to *make* their wives submit!) Children should obey their parents in everything because this pleases God (Colossians 3:20).

The greatest responsibility falls to the man. Someone has said that in any organization, 90 percent of what happens—or doesn't happen—results from the leadership. Man, you are the leader in your home. That's what the Bible says. Part of your responsibility as a Christian steward is to accept that leadership. If your family never prays together, that's your fault. If you don't go to church together, you're to blame. If Christian principles aren't taught and practiced in your home, you're accountable. What a tremendous privilege and opportunity you have to lead your family. Use your influence for the good. Mark your steps carefully. Be positive, show affection, share happiness.

You must be your family's model of dedication to God. First is your relationship with God. Then comes your wife, then your children, then other people. Remember: The most important thing a father can do for his children is to love their mother. That's true! Next to loving God, nothing is more important. Never allow your occupation, your hobby, or anything else to usurp the priority that belongs to your family. If you do, you are failing in your stewardship.

Don't exasperate your children (Ephesians 6:4). Don't condemn them; correct them lovingly. Be an encourager, not a discourager. Be their counselor, their helper, their guide, their advocate. And for the sake of their future give them time. TIME! Nothing can substitute for it. Give time. It's the only way you can determine the direction of your family. "Husbands, love your wives . . . . Fathers, do not exasperate your children; instead, bring them up in the training and instruction of the Lord." That's Scripture, and that's your stewardly obligation.

The Biblical model for the wife favors submission. Not because the woman is inferior in any way or should not have authority. But sometimes the buck must stop somewhere—not simply be passed back and forth. Wife, support your husband. He won't always be right, but don't condemn him for mistakes. He's responsible for his mistakes; you're responsible to stand by him. Help him in those areas where your experience and expertise surpass his. Share your burdens, your victories, your visions— then expect him to respond out of an attitude of sacrificial love (Ephesians 5:25).

Want to know what a model wife is like? Read what Paul says in Ephesians 5 and Colossians 3, but couple it with Proverbs 31:10-31. Not only is such a wife submissive, she is also excellent in business and domestic responsibilities, openly compassionate, joyful, and wise. And perhaps most importantly, she's deserving of reward (Proverbs 31:31).

What about the "kid" category? Scripture booms out one great directive: Obey! It's no New Testament revelation, either. That's always been God's policy. One of the Ten Commandments spells it out clearly (Exodus

20:12). Paul reiterates it (Colossians 3:20; Ephesians 6:1). " 'Honor your father and mother'—which is the first commandment with a promise—'that it may go well with you and that you may enjoy long life on the earth' " (Ephesians 6:2,3, NIV). Young person, weigh your actions and attitudes carefully. God expects you to maintain good relationships in the home. You'll be called to account just like your parents. Build strong bonds as a good steward of the family within which God has placed you.

On the Outside

Relationships. We've followed Paul in Colossians 3. He's dealt with the Christian and his relationships to himself, to fellow believers, and to his family. In the next chapter we will discuss Paul's teaching about employer-employee relationships. But now we will look at the Christian's relationships with non-Christians. Everyday we have to deal with people who are not Christians. Paul did too, and from his pen come three important traits that should characterize a Christian's relations with outsiders.

The first is *wisdom*. Colossians 4:5 admonishes believers to "walk in wisdom toward them that are without." "Walk" carries the idea of the Christian's daily course of life, the way he goes about his routine. There were many people in Colossae who claimed special spiritual wisdom, and some of them probably gave Paul and the church more trouble than anyone else! Paul's instruction is full of insight, saying, in effect, "Let those pseudo-wise men see real wisdom lived out in your lives!" Christians constantly are scrutinized, analyzed, and classified by outsiders. Talk is tested by walk. Be on guard to present no cause for tripping up someone. That's Paul's advice—both then and now.

Besides wisdom, demonstrate *readiness*. "Make the most of every opportunity" (Colossians 4:5, NIV). Every moment is a precious gift from God to be exploited and capitalized to the full. Paul's wording pictures the intense activity of the marketplace, of snapping up all the opportunities available at the present moment.

Demonstrate readiness for the Lord, but with *attractiveness*. "Let your speech be always with grace, seasoned with salt, that ye may know how ye ought to answer every man" (Colossians 4:6). Maintain pleasantness in relationships with unbelievers. Present the gospel attractively. Avoid soiling its message. Season your speech well, that it might provide a purifying, wholesome influence. Be wise, be ready, be attractive. That's the way to foster relationships with outsiders.

The Closing Curtain

Relationships are invaluable. They can endure through all the ups and downs life may bring. In fact, when life draws to a close, when health begins to fail and the importance of riches fades, relationships grow ever greater in value. Nothing outshines the beauty of true friendship, of a close-knit Christian family, of a church bound together in love, of a personal relationship with Jesus Christ.

Practice sound stewardship by cultivating and nurturing positive relationships while you have opportunity. You are called to the stewardship of relationships. They're part of that overall structure that forms your Christian economy. Manage your relationships well!

8

Workers or Shirkers?

I entered the building to behold a remarkable sight. There before me labored *five men* changing a burned-out light bulb! One struggled to change the bulb; one held the ladder; one handed the bulb to the "changer"; and two supervised. Five men to change a light bulb—that's classic joke material—but there it was, right before my eyes. But what made that situation doubly ridiculous was that it took place at a Christian institution.

That's an important point, because of all people, Christians should be careful and conscientious about their work. Obviously when it takes five men to change a light bulb, somebody's not being a good steward of his time or his employer's time. Christians must take extra care to be good stewards on the job, not taking advantage of their employer, not wasting time, but serving as if the Lord himself were in charge.

The average employee these days views work as a necessary evil, something to be endured. So often the challenge among workers is, Just how *little* can I do and still keep this job? Unfortunately, many get by with doing next to nothing day after day.

Feelings of frustration, disgust, anger, and bitterness develop so easily among workers. The good steward has to guard against them. God—not just your employer—expects accountability from you on the job. Don't expect happiness, fulfillment, promotions, or commendations from your work, your employer, or the Lord, if you fail in your stewardship on the job. Too many these days are shirkers instead of workers!

One of the Ten Commandments says, "Remember the sabbath day, to keep it holy" (Exodus 20:8). You know that; you probably learned it as a child. But sometimes we overlook the rest of that command: "Six days shalt thou *labor*, and do all thy *work*: but the seventh is the sabbath of the Lord thy God: in it thou shalt not do any work" (Exodus 20:9,10, emphasis mine). Catch the point? *Work* is commanded, too, just like the day of rest is. God expects honest, faithful work from His people, whether they be ancient Israelites or modern Christians.

Paul's Perspective

The apostle Paul perceived this clearly. In his letter to the Colossians he addresses the issue head-on. In Colossians 3:22 to 4:1 he writes concerning Christian slaves and masters. Granted, we don't have master-slave relationships these days, but the principles Paul sets forth also apply to the employer-employee relationship. Modern workers especially need to hear and heed what Paul says if they want even a measure of satisfaction on the job.

The keynote on which Paul begins his discussion is *responsibility*. Every employer or employee bears responsibilities he must fulfill. Christian workers have a responsibility to *avoid* doing some things, while, at the same time, they *must* do others. From the negative to the positive—that's how Paul so often works.

I once had a job working nights with a large crew of men. We had no official night foreman, no "company man" with authority over our crew. The boss usually went home about an hour after we started, so we worked almost our whole shift without his watchful eye. I was amazed at the change that came over those men whenever they saw the foreman's pickup leave. As long as he was around, they gave it their best, but when he left— what a change!

Those guys thrived on "eyeservice," as Paul calls it. That's working like a whirlwind while the boss is watching, but shirking responsibilities when he's not. That's working only to please men, being "menpleasers" (Colossians 3:22). Eyeservice, menpleasing—those are dispositions Christians should shun. We are not to work only when, and *because*, someone is watching. This principle applies to whatever kind of work you do, even school work!

Most people require incentives to work, something to prod them on, someone to check up on them, to make sure they give their best effort. But God's directions contradict that. He says, "You excel anyway, whether anybody's watching you or not!" The Christian steward should demonstrate a commitment to his work. That's a scriptural principle. And that commitment should be accompanied by obedience and honesty. Slovenly work on a Christian's part is a surefire symptom of shoddy stewardship.

Practice the Positive

Paul provides four positive standards to replace the negative. The first is obedience: "Servants, obey in all things your masters according to the flesh" (Colossians 3:22). Now remember these words originally had to do with master-slave relationships. Slaves were nothing more than property in most cases, to be used by their masters. If anyone had cause to rebel, to disobey, to complain, they did. If slaves were called to obedience to their earthly masters, certainly modern-day employees, who are obviously treated much better, should obey their employers.

Paul's not dealing with evil masters who flout Christian principles; different rules apply in that situation. Some bosses expect more from employees than Christians can give. You can think of obvious examples. But the point we need to distill from what Paul says is this: To the best of your ability, demonstrate obedience. If the boss says work starts at 8:00 A.M., then begin at 8:00 A.M.. Not 8:20, not 8:10, not even 8:02. Make it 8:00 sharp! If your coffee break is 10 minutes, then don't stretch it to 15 or 20. You might take some guff from fellow employees, but that's better than taking guff from your boss, or worse yet from God!

I worked in a very hot climate doing hard physical labor for several summers. As a treat for the employees, one of the men brought cold soda pop for the workers during their breaks. The problem: The drinks came in cans, and too many of the men just tossed the empty cans wherever they pleased when they finished. The work area became littered with them. Finally, the boss issued a directive: Either put the empty cans in the trash barrels, or the privilege of the soft drinks will end. The workers failed to obey, so the soft drinks stopped. A lack of obedience leads to a lack of privileges. The good Christian steward, to the best of his ability, obeys his employer.

On another occasion I worked in a small convenience store. I came to work one day to find that the manager had been fired. The reason: He'd been stealing merchandise. How easy it is to be dishonest in matters of work.

When you accept your wages from your employer, you

should be able to say in good conscience: "I have honestly done my very best at this job. I have fulfilled my responsibilities and have not taken advantage of my employer in any way." When you receive the report card at school, you should be able to say, "I have done my best."

"Whatsoever ye do, do it heartily, as to the Lord, and not unto men" (Colossians 3:23). Unless you give your best, you're not serving honestly and sincerely. You might just as well be stealing merchandise; you're cheating the one for whom you work.

Obedience, honesty, and now commitment. Whatever you do, do it heartily. That verse calls for not only honesty, but also commitment and dedication. Commitment doesn't mean spending all your time at work and neglecting home and family. Commitment doesn't mean setting aside your Christian principles. Paul's point is this: Whatever you do, and whenever you do it, make certain you give your best. That doesn't mean your employer will give you a raise, or even a word of praise. It simply means: Give it your best for God!

Finally, and perhaps the most Christian reason for being productive, work so you can share. "He who has been stealing must steal no longer, but must work, doing something useful with his own hands, that he may have something to share with those in need" (Ephesians 4:28, NIV).

Talk about going the second mile! Paul didn't stop with telling the thief to go straight, to earn his own living. He said work so you can help out others.

And don't think that was advice just for former thieves, a way to make up for their lives of crime. Paul told the church at Rome (without singling out thieves): "Let no debt remain outstanding, except the continuing debt to love one another" (Romans 13:8). And the debt of love is paid through action—put your money where your mouth is.

A Reassuring Word

An astronomer peered through his powerful telescope, carefully recording his observations of the sun. Dusk settled in, and the sun began to sink behind a hillside some 10 miles or so from the observatory. As the astronomer followed the course of the setting sun, he caught sight of two youngsters on the hillside. There, in the midst of an apple orchard, they were gathering apples. One of them climbed the trees and picked; the other stood watch. They were *stealing* the apples! As far as they knew, their activities were undetected. But there, 10 miles away, sat the astronomer watching their every move through his telescope.

Some employers behave as if no one really knows what they've been up to. Paul flatly contradicts that notion: "Masters, give unto your servants that which is just and equal; knowing that ye also have a Master in heaven" (Colossians 4:1). That declaration is both comforting and frightening at the same time. It's comforting to know that God will treat us fairly; He misses nothing. The employer stands answerable just as the employee does. That's a message of reassurance to the worker.

But, Mr. Employer, be sure you hear Paul's point clearly! His message can be frightening if you're failing in your responsibilities toward your employees. Practice sound scriptural labor management and there's no need for fear or uncertainty. Simply remember God watches your activities, so demonstrate your Christian concern even in the labor arena.

The Christian Key

The most important thing Paul says about work is in

Colossians 3:23,24. Take these words to heart because they are without question the key to Christian steward-ship on the job: "Whatsoever ye do, do it heartily, as to the Lord, and not unto men . . . for ye serve the Lord Christ."

Imagine those words written to slaves! Those short statements by Paul actually transformed the state of the slave in New Testament times, and they should transform the attitude of today's worker. What Paul says puts a heavenly value on ordinary toil. Those words make drudgery divine; they make monotony meaningful; they change boredom to beauty.

Have you ever noticed how the work of people is drastically affected by the one for whom they work? Our good friends bought a house. It was loaded with extra features, little finishing touches rarely found in houses these days. Why? Because the builder had originally constructed it as his own home. You see the point? The one for whom we work can make a world of difference in the nature of our labor.

In spirit, people cease to be slaves as soon as they begin to work for the Lord. The Christian's service be-comes sacred. That applies to every Christian in what-ever sphere he serves. It's not the government for whom you work; it's not the supermarket; it's not the depart-ment store; it's not the factory; it's not the corporation. You're not really working for any of these employers, Paul says. Not one of them is to be your "lord." You work for the Lord Jesus Christ. So let your work reflect that. Approach that job as a sacred service.

Reward or Reprimand

I'll never forget the many blessings we enjoyed in the first church we pastored. God used that congregation to enrich us in many ways. Among the greatest surprises and blessings were the Christmas gifts they gave us every year. The first one came as a complete shock. We simply had served that first year the best we could with the Lord's help. Then, what a boost to receive a special gift from those fine people, showing their appreciation and approval for what we had done!

Listen to Paul's words: "Whatsoever ye do, do it heartily, to the Lord, and not unto men; knowing that of the Lord ye shall receive the reward of the inheritance" (Colossians 3:23,24). Something more awaits the Christian who practices good stewardship on the job, something like that special Christmas gift we received. God has a reward in store for you. There's something more than just the wages your employer pays you. There's something more than the profit you make in your business. Your motives, your sincerity, your commitment, your honesty, your faithfulness—they all affect the inheritance the Lord has in store. If you work well, Paul says, Christ, your real master, will reward you.

But then there's the other side of the coin: "He that doeth wrong shall receive for the wrong which he hath done; and there is no respect of persons" (Colossians 3:25). If you do wrong—whether as master or slave, employer or employee—you will be repaid in kind. If you render shoddy service to your employer, if you work halfheartedly in school, if you mistreat employees, you're really doing these things to the Lord. A time of recompense awaits, when the scales will be balanced. Sooner or later, poor service will come back to haunt you!

Perform your daily activities with a new realization. Whatever you do, you are in the Lord's service. That should provide your motivation. Your service to the Lord is not limited to what you do on Sunday or Wednesday or any other day of the week. It's not even limited to certain kinds of activities. The Christian is constantly in the Lord's service. Wise stewardship reckons on that.

A scriptural economy is a *total* system, encompassing every aspect of life. Make your vocation an integral part of that system—hand it to God. He already views it as under His jurisdiction. What a difference it will make in your life when you do too.

9

Where Are You Headed?

Jesus told a strange story about a dishonest manager. The manager was called to account for mishandling his master's wealth. "What is this I hear about you?" his master asked. "Give an account of your management, because you cannot be manager any longer" (Luke 16:2, NIV).

Contemplating his future and the mess he'd gotten himself into, the manager reasoned: " 'What shall I do now? My master is taking away my job. I'm not strong enough to dig, and I'm ashamed to beg—I know what I'll do so that, when I lose my job here, people will welcome me into their houses' " (Luke 16:3,4, NIV).

The manager called his master's debtors and proceeded to reduce their debts by considerable sums. He cut a debt of 800 gallons of olive oil in half. He reduced a debt of 1,000 bushels of wheat to 800. Surprisingly, when the manager completed his underhanded tactics, his master commended him. Listen to the conclusion Jesus attaches to His story:

> The master commended the dishonest manager because he had acted shrewdly. For the people of this world are more shrewd in dealing with their own kind than are the people of the light (Luke 16:8, NIV).

That story is certainly one of Jesus' more unusual ones.

A *dishonest* manager becomes a model for Christ's followers. Why? How? Obviously not because of his dishonesty or his unscrupulous business practices. What makes him an example for Christians is simply this: As he faced his future, he made plans with a wisdom and a shrewdness that often put God's people to shame. He saw the necessity of organizing the present with a view to the future.

Someone once said, "My interest is in the future because I intend to spend the rest of my life there." The future *is* important, and God's call to you as a Christian steward is to be a wise manager of that future by planning with God in mind. What do you see for yourself as you peer down the pathway of time 5, 10, 20, even 30 years from now?

Granted, Jesus might return during that period and all of our planning would be overridden. But while we are living on earth God expects us to assess where we're headed. Planning with God in mind—that's such a significant, though often overlooked, aspect of Christian stewardship.

Wisdom That Works

The wisdom in the letter of James speaks to the issue of wise Christian planning. James details several planning principles every Christian needs to master and practice. The first deals with a problem of epidemic proportions these days.

Can you guess what it is? No, it's not some contagious disease carried by bacteria. It's not a sickness a physician can innoculate you against. Rather, it's a spiritual problem, a problem perhaps best classified as rebellion. James says, "Now listen, you who say, 'Today or tomorrow we will go to this or that city, spend a year there, carry on business and make money . . .' " (James 4:13, NIV).

Money is not the problem addressed by James. No, the problem is a self-centered, independent attitude in planning: "I will go here. I will go there. I will do this. I will do that. I will make money. I will . . . , I will . . . , I will . . . !

"Wow!" you say, "that sounds just like people in our world today—like the unsaved, worldly people I know." That's right; it does. But sadly, it also sounds like many Christians—churchgoers who fail to see the intricate connection between their confession of Christ as Saviour and the control of Christ in their lives, people so engrossed in their own personal plans that any thought of a divine plan for their lives is shoved aside, people who believe that religion—church attendance, public prayer, offerings—is the sum total of God's plan and concern for their lives.

To these people—to Christians, to churchgoers—James shouts: "Now listen: Avoid that attitude of arrogance. It's an offense to God!"

Wake Up!

"Why, you do not even know what will happen tomorrow. What is your life? You are a mist that appears for a little while and then vanishes" (James 4:14, NIV). It's time to wake up and face the facts, James says. Stop living as if God doesn't exist. And realize this—you don't *know* what the future holds and you may not live to see it. That's not pleasant to think about, but it's the truth. We make all our big plans, like the farmer who insisted on building bigger and better barns for his bumper crop (Luke 12:13-21), then find ourselves facing eternity long before we anticipated and all our plans crumble.

Genesis 11 preserves a curious story about a group of fellows who planned to build a magnificent tower as a monument to themselves. You can almost hear their excited planning sessions: " 'Come, let us build ourselves a city, with a tower that reaches to the heavens, so that we may make a name for ourselves and not be scattered over the face of the whole earth' " (Genesis 11:4, NIV).

What knowledge they had, knowledge of building techniques; knowledge of architecture; knowledge of social institutions, communications. And what importance they had: "We deserve recognition!" they exclaimed. "We should have a monument erected to ourselves!" So they began constructing a tower to demonstrate their knowledge and proclaim their greatness.

Then, as Genesis 11:5-8 says, the Lord "came down" to see what was happening. It was not a monument to Him that He saw. It was not one of those good works that inspire others to "glorify [the] Father . . . in heaven." God saw a project of pride, inspired by man, reflecting man.

That's an interesting story, but what's the point? you ask. The point is this: James says Christians are guilty of the same kind of arrogance. If you try to build the tower of your life using any plans other than God's, don't be surprised if it doesn't get completed. And if it does get completed, don't be surprised if it doesn't satisfy you. You see, your life is really fruitless until you live it according to the divine plan.

The Bible has other similar pictures of man's building plans without God: the "great Babylon" of Nebuchadnezzar, a house built on sand, bigger barns for more wealth. All of them have an ending similar to the Genesis story—the judgment of God. Take a minute to read the conclusion of the story in Genesis 11, especially verses 5-9, then give some thought to how that speaks to you right now.

Here Today, Gone Tomorrow

Outside the Bible we can find more stories of successful failures, people who accomplished much in their lifetimes only to have eternity devalue the results.

One of these people is Ozymandias, Ramses II of Egypt. Whether or not he is the pharaoh who would not let Moses' people go, history says he was an overbearing and ambitious ruler. He wanted to recover Egypt's Asiatic empire. But he was stymied by the Hittites. Nevertheless, according to Diodorus Siculus, the Greek historian of the first century B.C., the largest statue in Egypt carried this inscription: "I am Ozymandias, king of kings; if anyone wishes to know what I am and where I lie, let him surpass me in some of my exploits."

Perhaps it was this very inscription that inspired the early 19th-century English poet Shelly. Just picture the last five lines.

Ozymandias

I met a traveler from an antique land
Who said: Two vast and trunkless legs of stone
Stand in the desert . . . Near them, on the sand,
Half sunk, a shattered visage lies, whose frown,
And wrinkled lip, and sneer of cold command,
Tell that its sculptor well those passions read
Which yet survive, stamped on these lifeless things,
The hand that mocked them, and the heart that fed;
And on the pedestal these words appear:
"My name is Ozymandias, king of kings:
Look on my works, ye Mighty, and despair!"
Nothing beside remains. Round the decay
Of that colossal wreck, boundless and bare
The lone and level sands stretch far away.

James wants us to know that life passes before we realize it; it's a vapor that disappears with the midmorning sun. We must not fool ourselves about our significance with our own "great" plans. If we do, our legacy will be as empty and as foolish-sounding as Ozymandias'.

Formula for Success

Fortunately, James spells out an alternative. Instead of boasting about all your great plans "you ought to say, 'If it is the Lord's will, we will live and do this or that'" (James 4:15, NIV). Shift the focus of your life, especially your plans for the future, from yourself and your dreams and goals to God and His plans. Adjust your coming and going, your buying and selling, your moving and staying—adjust everything—to conform to His plan.

Submitting the future to the lordship of Jesus Christ—handing it to God—that's what James is talking about. God's will must take precedence over everything else as you consider the days, weeks, months, and years that lie ahead. You must formulate your future according to God's plan, not someone else's, refusing to give in to the pressures that surround you: pressure from peers who say you should do this or who expect you to do that; pressure to go after wealth, money, possessions; the pressure of pride that says, "I wanna be something big in the eyes of the world!" You need steel in your spine to stand against those pressures.

John 21 preserves a beautiful encounter between the resurrected Jesus and Peter. Three times Jesus asks Peter if he loves Him, and each time Peter says yes. After Peter's third response, Jesus predicts that when Peter is old he will stretch out his hands, and someone else will dress him and lead him where he doesn't want to go.

Jesus said this to indicate the kind of death by which Peter would glorify God. Then he said to him, "Follow me!"

Peter turned and saw that the disciple whom Jesus loved was following them. . . . When Peter saw him, he asked, "Lord, what about him?"

Jesus answered, "If I want him to remain alive until I return, what is that to you? You must follow me" (John 21:19-22, NIV).

Did you catch what Jesus said? "It doesn't matter what My plan for somebody else is. You just make sure you follow the way I've prescribed for *you*." Jesus insisted that Peter make Him lord of his future. That's what He expects from you too!

Following the Call

A farmer's hen hatched three wild duck eggs, and the ducklings made their home on the farmer's 2-acre lake. With the fall, the farmer anticipated the departure of his now full-grown wild ducks. Other ducks had made his lake their home, too, and he knew when the time came all of them would rise together to begin their long migration southward.

But the old farmer hit upon a scheme. Every day for 3 weeks he threw out corn for the ducks. They loved it, and they got fat and lazy. The time came to migrate, but the ducks were so used to the free corn, they simply forgot to leave. The desire for that free corn stifled the urge to take to the sky, the urge they knew they should follow. Instead, they made that 2-acre lake their home.

James says in 4:17: "Anyone, then, who knows the good he ought to do and doesn't do it, sins"(NIV). That is a shocking, profound statement. Do you realize what it means? It means, if God has shared with you a portion of His plan for your life and you have rejected it, then you've sinned. You're no better than Jonah. God commissioned him to go to Nineveh and preach. But Jonah refused and got himself into all kinds of hot water. If you've rejected God's plan, you're likely to get into lots of trouble too.

What James says is that God looks just as harshly on sins of *omission* as on sins of *commission*. Sins of commission are the wrong acts we commit, things we do that we shouldn't. Sins of omission are the things we do not do that we know we should. Seeing a need and failing to meet it. Knowing God's will and failing to follow it. Witnessing a wrong and failing to correct it. "Anyone, then, who knows the good he ought to do and doesn't do it, sins." James couldn't have said it more clearly!

A Critical Question

Could the way you spend your future be sinful? If you are not following God's plan for your life, that's exactly what James says your future will be. Have you ever thought about that?

If you don't follow God's plan for your life, you are not practicing good Christian stewardship. You are not managing your future according to a scriptural economy.

Make certain you plan for the future with God's desires as top priority. You've got to hand your future to God. Make Him leader and lord of your life from this moment forward. Plan your future openly. Plan for your own personal welfare and the welfare of your family and loved ones. But most importantly, plan for the fulfillment of God's calling. Do it in the big and the little things. It *is* important where you live, where you work, where you go to college, who you marry, whether you witness to those to whom God leads you, etc. God is concerned about these things.

Be open to God's leading. You can't be a good Christian steward without bringing your plans under the Saviour's control. Your scriptural economy must be a total system, one that includes even your future. The Spanish language has a farewell that sums it up well: *¡Vaya con Dios!* "Go with God!"

10

Going, Going, Gone!

We were set. We had a cashier's check for several thousand dollars, all of our belongings loaded on a truck, and a call to join the faculty of a college in the Midwest. The wheels were turning; we were excited about what the future held. With a vision in our hearts, we headed east to follow the Lord's call.

The balloon burst quickly. My salary was small, too small for a family of four to live on, so we invested a large portion of the money we had earned from the sale of our home. However, in less than a year, thousands of dollars had disappeared, lost through hasty, unwise investments. How could this have happened so suddenly, almost viciously, to people merely trying to make ends meet? I'm still not sure I know the answer to that question. But our experience illustrates one unpleasant truth: People can lose money—sometimes large sums of money—almost as quickly as you can blink!

A Spiritual Matter

Finances—the first thought that comes to mind when the subject of stewardship surfaces. And how very important finances are! So many people these days get upset whenever the matters of money and religion are mixed, as if the two had nothing to do with one another. How foolish! Assuming the Gospels accurately reflect the relative amount of teaching Jesus did on various subjects during His earthly ministry, we have to admit that He had a lot to say about money and the handling of it.

In light of that, how can people contend that Christianity and finances are not to mix? That's a mystery! Well, actually, it's probably not so much a mystery as it is a self-indictment on the part of poor stewards. Far too many churchgoers search for innovative ways to skirt their financial responsibilities to the work of the Lord, just like many religious leaders in Jesus' day who made high-sounding confessions but failed to follow through in tangible ways.

It is a little more understandable that non-Christians cannot make sense of and have no appreciation for the role of finances in the church and the life of the Christian.

My father had not been a Christian long when, at work on a Monday morning, a coworker my father had encouraged to attend church jovially slapped him on the back and blurted out, "Well, how much did that preacher soak you for this weekend?"

That's a blatantly unscriptural, unchristian, uninformed point of view, but it's the understanding of the unsaved. How clearly such an attitude confirms the words of Paul: "The natural man receiveth not the things of the Spirit of God: for they are foolishness unto him: neither can he know them, because they are spiritually discerned" (1 Corinthians 2:14). That's right, the way a Christian views and handles money and material possessions is a *spiritual* matter. That's why the non-Christian can't understand the way Christians "throw their money away" by giving it to the work of the Kingdom. The believer and unbeliever simply are not on the same wavelength!

Check Your Frequency

Have you ever tried to tune in a particular radio station without knowing its frequency? You've got no choice but to turn the dial from one end to the other, enduring the scratches and screeches and pops and whines, until you finally tune in the familiar station you enjoy. You've got to be on the right wavelength. You've got to tune out all the static, all those other voices competing to be heard. And that's exactly what Christians must do when it comes to financial matters. To be good stewards, we must tune out the static of the world's advice and tune in what Scripture says. The Bible should be our financial adviser. It's got plenty of principles to guide us in handling our assets, but we must put them into practice.

Jesus often taught about money. In fact, in three different stories recorded in the Gospels, Jesus summarizes the three basic options open to all of us when it comes to managing our money. The key is tuning in to what He says, and then recognizing where we fit among those three alternatives.

Eat, Drink, and Be Merry

Let's take another look at the Prodigal Son (see Luke 15). It's one of Jesus' most famous parables. A young son went to his father and requested his inheritance. "I'm gonna live a little, see what life's all about!"

His father granted his son the inheritance, and not many days later, Jesus says, the son "gathered all together, and took his journey into a far country, and there wasted his substance on riotous living" (Luke 15:13). He spent everything, probably living like a king as long as his money lasted.

Fortunately, his predicament got so bad that the former carouser woke up to how far down he'd fallen. The memory of his father's house and all the benefits he had enjoyed there finally overcame him. He cried out in sorrow and determined to return home, hoping his father would accept him back as a hired servant.

The beauty of the story is the picture of the father, who represents God, waiting lovingly and patiently for his son to return. And when he sees him, he welcomes him, reinstates him, and celebrates his return.

The matter of money and money management surfaces in an interesting manner in the parable. The Prodigal Son received his inheritance from his father. Now that should reinforce a truth already firmly implanted in your heart: God is the real owner and bestower of all you have. Never forget that! What the son received actually belonged to his father. The son obviously didn't look at it that way. Unfortunately, neither do a lot of Christians.

But the son was also guilty of believing another common fallacy: Happiness comes when you have plenty of money and can spend it any way you please, any time you please. Have you ever dreamed of having enough money to buy anything and everything you ever wanted? Solomon got to follow through on such a fantasy. Centuries before the Prodigal he wrote: "I denied myself nothing my heart desired; I refused my heart no pleasure . . . . Nothing was gained" (Ecclesiastes 2:10, NIV).

Do you recall the "unalienable rights" man is supposedly endowed with, according to the Declaration of Independence? "Life, liberty and the pursuit of happiness."

Why didn't Thomas Jefferson write simply "happiness," that man has the right to happiness?

Because he was wise enough to realize that politically happiness could not be provided—only its *pursuit* could.

The Prodigal pursued it with money. Today, many people continue to take the same route, or fantasize about having enough money to do that. But don't delude yourself into thinking that a bundle of money brings happiness and contentment. It doesn't! The young man in the story found that out real quick. Using money to eat, drink, and be merry loses its appeal when it means sacrificing other necessities of life. Squandering money is obviously not what God has in mind for Christians. Happiness and contentment can't be purchased, as the Prodigal Son quickly discovered.

Hold, Hoard, and Hallow

A few chapters earlier in Luke, Jesus tells another story, this time about a man very unlike the squandering son. In fact, he's almost the exact opposite. Instead of spending, he grasps. Instead of squandering, he hoards. Maybe you remember the story.

A farmer's land yielded abundant crops, so abundant, in fact, that he had nowhere to put everything. But he soon hit upon a solution:

> This will I do, I will pull down my barns, and build greater; and there will I bestow all my fruits and my goods. And I will say to my soul, Soul, thou hast much goods laid up for many years; take thine ease, eat, drink, and be merry (Luke 12:18,19).

Now the farmer may sound like the Prodigal Son with his plan to eat, drink, and be merry, but he never got the chance to arrive at that point. "God said unto him, Thou fool, this night thy soul shall be required of thee: then whose shall those things be, which thou hast provided?" (Luke 12:20).

Do you know the story of Hetty Green? She died in 1916. In one bank alone she left $31,400,000. She ate her oatmeal cold because it cost money to heat it. Her son lost his leg because it took her awhile to find a *free* clinic. That's what the *Guinness Book of World Records* (1971-72) says—under "Greatest Miser." She was something like the rich farmer Jesus told about. Such people think money is to be hoarded, guarded, grasped; they never have enough.

What's wrong with that kind of money management? For one thing, the farmer had the attitude that he himself was responsible for the great harvest he was reaping and that his tremendous yields would continue. He showed no concern for the One who sends the rain or grants the sunshine. He left God out of the picture.

Besides that, he was something like the Prodigal Son in thinking that the material side of life was of far greater importance than anything else. He lived in the material realm only. Now if that doesn't speak to contemporary western society, nothing in Scripture will! People may not be building bigger barns these days, but they're sure building bigger houses, bigger garages for their cars and boats, and bigger bank accounts to ensure a life of ease and enjoyment in the years ahead. Money, possessions, financial security—they're all hallowed these days, as if they create a heaven on earth.

Now, don't misunderstand: No one is saying that Christians shouldn't plan for their future and the future of their families. That's not the point. The problem is overemphasizing the material side of life until the spiritual is squeezed out. That was the rich man's greatest problem, and that's why he's addressed as a fool.

Take time to inventory your own attitudes toward money and possessions. Make a personal commitment right now never to end up as a "rich fool." "All That Thrills My Soul [Is Jesus]," that's the title and chorus line of an old gospel song sung in many churches. But too many people would sing those words much more honestly if "Jesus" were deleted and "Money" inserted! Be careful not to become one of them.

You've Gotta Hand It to God

Two parables, two bad examples, two graspers. They didn't realize that ultimately everything comes from God and belongs to God. Matthew 25 preserves Jesus' story of the talents. Before journeying to a far country, a man called his servants and handed his goods over to them for safekeeping. He gave one man five talents, another man two talents, and another, one. Then he left on his trip.

Now a talent was a unit of money estimated at more than a thousand dollars by today's standards. So these sums were nothing to wink at; considerable responsibility fell on those servants.

Jesus says both the man with five talents and the man with two talents took the money and invested it; when their master returned, they presented him with a 100-percent increase in his money. The man with five talents returned ten; the man with two returned four. But the man who had received one talent failed in his responsibility. He took the money, buried it, and let it lie dormant while his master was absent. Because of his profitless return, the servant received rebuke, his one talent was taken from him, and he was cast out from the presence of the master.

In this parable lies the clue to proper money management for the Christian. There are three options: Like the Prodigal Son, you can squander your money until you have nothing left. Or like the rich fool, you can hoard it, never putting it to work, never using it to help others or to enlarge or enrich the Lord's work. Or like the good stewards in this last story, you can put it to work for God and for good.

To the stewards faithful in their handling of the master's money, the master says: "Well done, thou good and faithful servant: thou hast been faithful over a few things, I will make thee ruler over many things: enter thou into the joy of the Lord" (Matthew 25:21,23).

Putting money to work for the benefit of the Master— that's what the servants did to receive such high commendation. Money became a proving ground for them, a test of their faithfulness and abilities. Having passed the test, they were promoted to higher levels of service. Remember that the next time you consider squandering or hoarding the material blessings God has bestowed on you. You're being examined!

A Parting Plea

The apostle Paul pulled no punches in his letters, and he obviously knew of the problems that surround money. Listen to his wise counsel to the young pastor Timothy at the close of his first letter:

> Godliness with contentment is great gain. For we brought nothing into the world, and we can take nothing out of it. But if we have food and clothing, we will be content with that. People who want to get rich fall into temptation and a trap and into many foolish and harmful desires that plunge men into ruin and destruction. For the love of money is a root of all kinds of evil. Some people, eager for money, have wandered from the faith and pierced themselves with many griefs.
>
> But you, man of God, flee from all this, and pursue righteousness, godliness, faith, love, endurance and gentleness (1 Timothy 6:6-11, NIV).

11

It's Better To Give

Hadrian assumed leadership of the Roman Empire early in the second century. In the year 135 (about 100 years after the death and resurrection of Jesus) a man named Aristides sent a letter to Emperor Hadrian. His subject: some people known as Christians. Listen to the way he describes them:

> They walk in all humility and kindness, and falsehood is not among them. They love one another. They do not refuse to help widows. They rescue the orphans from violence. He who has gives ungrudgingly to him who lacks. If they see a stranger, they take him home and entertain him as a brother. When one of their poor passes from this world, any one of them who sees it provides for his burial according to his ability. Truly this is a new people and there is something divine in them.[1]

Isn't that interesting! What made these early Christians so noteworthy was the way they gave of what they had to others. This responsibility has always rested on the people of God. And yet it presents such a stumbling-block to so many Christians. For some people money and possessions are too precious to part with. But the person who is able to give to God and God's work out of a cheerful, willing heart is a candidate for tremendous blessing. There's no question about it: To be a good steward in the kingdom of God, you'd better be ready and willing to anoint your assets! That means being will-ing to consecrate them, to allow the power of God to work through them. Your assets carry tremendous po-tential for good, if you will simply unleash it.

Maybe you've given faithfully to the Lord's work for years. If so, you can probably testify to God's faithfulness in meeting your needs. Or maybe you've never taken this important step of stewardship. Wherever you are in your journey, you need to understand what Scripture teaches on this subject. How should you give? Let's see what the Bible says.

Use Your Head

Have you ever had to do something and you had no idea *why* you were doing it? Sure, I have too. But for-tunately, God seldom asks anyone to do anything without giving some explanation of what's going on. That's true even in the matter of giving. High on the list of answers to the question, "How should you give?" is this response: You should give knowledgeably. In other words, you need to understand what you're doing and what you're not doing when you give to the work of God.

Five things are extremely important along these lines. First, you need to understand that giving is God's plan for the Christian. Listen to just a few passages from Scripture: "Bring ye all the tithes into the storehouse" (Malachi 3:10). "On the first day of the week, each one of you should set aside a sum of money" (1 Corinthians 16:2, NIV). Jesus said, "Give, and it shall be given unto you" (Luke 6:38). We like to emphasize the last part of that statement, but we dare not leave out the command to give. Giving is *God's* plan for you, not mine or any other person's. God commands it. You'd be wise to listen.

Second, sharing is God's way. "He did not even keep

back his own Son, but offered him for us all! He gave us his Son—will he not also freely give us all things?" (Romans 3:32, TEV). And as Jesus instructed His disciples, "Freely ye have received, freely give" (Matthew 10:8).

Even if those verses relate only to spiritual matters, the following certainly cover the material side of giving:

"Share with God's people who are in need" (Romans 12:13, NIV).

"Be rich in good deeds, . . . generous and willing to share" (1 Timothy 6:18, NIV).

"As we have . . . opportunity, let us do good unto all men" (Galatians 6:10).

A third principle is this: Giving is not only commanded by God, but is commended by Him as well. As Jesus indicated (Luke 6:38), we get a return on it. Jesus also said it's more blessed to give than to receive (Acts 20:35). In Luke 21:3,4 Jesus watched a poor little widow put money into a collection box, and He commended her for it. Giving is a good thing in God's sight.

This fourth point is paramount: Giving is an act of worship. Not just any giving, mind you, but giving done in the proper spirit, with proper motives and attitudes. Perhaps nowhere in Scripture is this better illustrated than in Deuteronomy 26:1-11. Take a moment to read this beautiful passage. Having recounted all that God had done for him, the man of God said, "Now I bring the firstfruits of the soil that you, O Lord, have given me." Then the worshiper was instructed:

> Place the basket before the Lord your God and bow down before him. And you and the Levites and the aliens among you shall rejoice in all the good things the Lord your God has given to you and your household (Deuteronomy 26:10,11, NIV).

Giving is an act of worship, symbolizing your acknowledgment of God as the true owner and provider of all you enjoy.

A fifth principle (in a more negative tone): giving of your assets can never substitute for fulfilling other Christian responsibilities. In other words, you can't buy your way out of other responsibilities God places upon you. Matthew 23:23 preserves an important rebuke by Jesus aimed at the religious leaders of His day:

> Woe unto you, scribes and Pharisees, hypocrites! for ye pay tithe of mint and anise and cummin, and have omitted the weightier matters of the law, judgment, mercy and faith: these ought ye to have done, and not to leave the other undone.

Jesus' point is simply this: The giving of your assets is great, but it can never substitute for neglecting other areas of responsibility. God's favor can never be purchased with your money.

By all means, when you give, give knowledgeably. Use your head; understand what Scripture teaches about giving, and then follow through faithfully.

Be Aboveboard

Acts 5 recounts the sobering story of a couple named Ananias and Sapphira. They sold a piece of property, brought the money from the sale, and placed it at the apostles' feet—under the pretense that they were giving the entire amount. But they had secretly withheld a portion of the money for themselves. Take a look at Acts 5:3-10. Can you imagine both Ananias and Sapphira being struck dead, and the shock that must have sent through the congregation and the community? God wasn't messing around! If that won't put the fear of the Lord into people, nothing will.

Now, understand this: It was *not* because Ananias and Sapphira had retained a portion of the money for themselves that God judged them. No. It was their pretense (read verses 3 and 4 carefully). The lesson is this: When you give, give honestly. There's no need for pretense. If your motive in giving is to impress other people you might as well not give at all. Make honesty in giving a priority.

Along with honesty, practice regularity in giving. Time and again in the Old Testament, God prescribed *regular* giving on the part of His people (see Deuteronomy 14:22-29; 26). Paul instructed the Corinthian Christians to set aside a sum of money "upon the first day of the week" so that when he arrived no special offerings would be necessary (1 Corinthians 16:2). Our God is a God of order, and part of that order is regularity in the giving of His people.

"Oh," some say, "but I give as God leads. I'm not bound by some legalistic formula. I give as the Holy Spirit prompts me."

Shades of spiritual arrogance seep through the cracks of those claims. The implication is this: "I'm more spiritual than those 'regular givers.' They're in bondage to legalistic formulas." The Bible says that Christians are free, yes, but no Christian is free to break the laws and teachings of Scripture. They teach regularity in giving.

Suppose an employer came up to his worker after he had labored for a month, handed him a paycheck, and said: "Oh, by the way, you should know that I don't pay regularly. I just pay as I feel led. You'll get paid when I feel prompted."

Now that's ridiculous. Not one of us would put up with that. We need the dependability of a regular income. An employer who practiced those tactics would more than likely be a cheapskate who just wanted to keep all his money for himself!

Could that be what's wrong with Christians who proudly proclaim, "I just give as the Spirit leads me"? More often than not, that high-sounding statement is just a cover for a covetous spirit. They might as well say, "I *won't* give regularly because I want it for myself." Guard yourself against that kind of covetousness.

Be Generous

My parents never had much money, so whenever they undertook a project, funds were always short. I'll never forget my father and me tearing down an old barrack, salvaging the lumber, and eventually building a very respectable garage out of it. It fell to me to pull the old nails out of that lumber. The boards were old and dry and brittle; the nails, rusty and worn. I was just a youngster, and I had a terrible time trying to pull those nails with just a claw hammer.

The answer was a crowbar. I would latch on to those nails with that bar, then throw all my strength and weight against them. Most of them would literally *scream* as I extracted them from those old boards. They were so set, so secure; they'd been there so long, they weren't about to let anybody remove them without putting up a good fight and complaining about it as loudly as possible. If you've ever pulled nails, you know exactly the irritating noise I'm talking about.

When it comes to giving, some Christians are just like those old, rusty nails. Prying them loose from their money produces screams of agony. Paul encourages Christians to practice generosity, and he says concerning giving, "If the *willingness* is there, the gift is acceptable according to what one has" (2 Corinthians 8:12, NIV, emphasis mine). Be careful, because the converse is also true: If the willingness is *not* there, the gift is *not* acceptable. If you don't give willingly, you might as well not give at all.

The desire of God is for His people to give not just willingly but even cheerfully. "God loveth a cheerful giver" (2 Corinthians 9:7). Now that should say something about the grumpy, growling, grumbling giver, too! God's model is one who gives cheerfully, out of a heart overflowing with joy and thanksgiving for the abundance God has bestowed.

Ecclesiastes talks about casting your bread upon the water and then having it return to you later (Ecclesiastes 11:1). Paul, in a context concerned with giving, writes of the law of sowing and reaping: "He which soweth sparingly shall reap also sparingly; and he which soweth bountifully shall reap also bountifully" (2 Corinthians 9:6). Jesus said we should give, and when we do, we'll find men giving back to us "a good measure, pressed down, shaken together and running over. . . . For with the measure you use, it will be measured to you" (Luke 6:38, NIV).

All of that's pretty plain. Give generously; receive generously. Give little; receive little. But the encouragement you need to hear is this: As you give, you can expect God's blessing! Give with vision, anticipating God's goodness to come your way. Expect your generosity to return to you. Now, that may not mean material returns. Material prosperity isn't promised for foolishly giving everything away. But God will send blessings in response to wise, honest generosity. Expect your *needs*, not necessarily your *wants*, to be met through God's faithfulness.

But How Much Is Enough?

Now the really tough question: Not just *how* should I

give, but *how much* should I give? Unfortunately, too many Christians phrase that question a little differently. They would rather ask, How *little* may I give? That reflects a woefully inadequate appreciation of the blessings of God.

In anticipation of his personal visit, Paul encouraged each Corinthian Christian to set aside a sum of money on the first day of the week *in keeping with his income* (1 Corinthians 16:2). Sounds like Paul expected each Corinthian to give a certain percentage of his income. In fact, that's precisely what he expected—and that's what God expects of all believers.

But now the heavy question: What is the percentage to be? How much should I give? Take note that Paul didn't put any limits on that percentage; it's open-ended. He was encouraging generosity. Surely he couldn't have expected anything less than 10 percent. That's right, the tithe. That's all the word *tithe* means, 10 percent.

Throughout the Old Testament, God commands His people to tithe, to give one-tenth of their income to Him.

"Aw, come off it!" some say. "Jesus never said we should tithe. That's law; we're under grace!"

You believe Jesus freed us from the Law. You do well. Otherwise, as Paul indicates in Galatians, gentiles would never have received the Holy Spirit (Galatians 3:2). When no man could, Jesus himself fulfilled the Law. But take a closer look at the expectations of the gospel: "Love each other as I have loved you" (John 15:12, NIV). "Love is the fulfillment of the law" (Romans 13:8-10, NIV).

As a matter of fact, as Dr. Stanley Horton points out, "the Law of Moses was never intended to be taken merely as a set of rules. God meant it to be the response of the heart to His grace that delivered Israel out of Egypt and brought them to Himself (Exodus 19:4-6; 20:2). God's people were to love Him first with all their heart, soul, and might, and then keep the words of His command-ments" (Deuteronomy 6:4-6).[2]

Jesus reaffirmed the command to love God completely (Matthew 22:37-40). And he said, "By this shall all men know that ye are my disciples, if ye have love one to another" (John 13:35).

What is one supreme expression of love? Giving! The person who truly loves does not draw the line at *what* he gives. Certainly he does not hold back his money. If he loves things, he puts his money in things. If he loves pleasure, he spends his money on pleasure. If he loves women, he showers them with what money can buy. If he loves God, he—

The saying is true: If God truly has a man's heart, He has his pocketbook. Does it make sense that a person under grace will give *less* than a person under law?

It May Even Hurt!

As he looked up, Jesus saw the rich putting their gifts into the temple treasury. He also saw a poor widow put in two very small copper coins. "I tell you the truth," he said, "this poor widow has put in more than all the others. All these people gave their gifts out of their wealth; but she out of her poverty put in all she had to live on" (Luke 21:1-4, NIV).

Does that sound like an endorsement on giving nothing? Does that sound like a recommendation to abandon tithing? Hardly! If anything, Jesus places a greater responsibility on His followers. He calls us to give sacrificially.

Paul repeats the same principle when he writes concerning the giving of the churches in Macedonia:

Out of the most severe trial, their overflowing joy and their extreme poverty welled up in rich generosity. For I

104

testify that they gave as much as they were able, and even beyond their ability (2 Corinthians 8:2,3, NIV).

They gave *beyond their ability*. That's sacrificial giving. And as the writer of Hebrews notes, "With such sacrifices God is pleased" (13:16, NIV).

What examples of sound, sacrificial stewardship Scripture provides! Purpose in your own life to make giving your assets to God a top priority. Then anticipate the working of God in your life. Expect to reap, as you sow faithfully.

----

[1]G. Ernest Thomas, *Spiritual Life Through Tithing* (Nashville: Tidings, 1953), p. 34.

[2]Stanley M. Horton, "The Law of Christ," *The Youth Leader*, April 1976, pp. 3, 4.

12

Get In Uniform

World War II, Pacific theater. My father operated heavy equipment, and on this particular day, he was bulldozing for an airstrip on one of the islands. Unexpectedly, he looked up to see enemy aircraft close by. Immediately he cut the engine, jumped to the ground, and crawled under the bulldozer. In that situation, he was concerned for his physical welfare, so he availed himself of the best protection he could find. Fortunately, the enemy didn't attack.

Lots of Christians try to stand against the enemy's attacks without any protection. They stand alone, exposed, out in the open, foolishly assuming they can ward off the enemy on their own. But the Bible says God has provided the believer with a source of strength and protection. When the enemy descends, sending forth a barrage of fiery darts, God expects the Christian to be ready to withstand his attacks.

Being a good steward means using the resources the Lord makes available. That includes appropriating the armor of the Lord. No football player enters the contest in street clothes. He needs the protection of pads, helmet, and all the other equipment made for playing the game. To play without them invites serious injury, perhaps even death.

The Christian fights a battle. The Bible says he's engaged in warfare. Warriors must prepare themselves. The good steward takes advantage of the available armaments and uses them wisely. That's what Paul encourages in Ephesians 6:10-18, a passage rich in imagery. Keep your Bible handy; we'll look at some important truths from that passage in the rest of this chapter.

I grew up in an area where the lumber industry dominated the economy, so our little community held a celebration every summer called the Loggers Jamboree. One of the most exciting parts of that celebration was a contest called the log roll. A large log was floated in the water, and two contestants mounted it, one on each end. The objective was to remain standing on that log while making your opponent fall into the water. It called for some fancy footwork, a quick turn here, a rapid twist there. It required constant awareness of the moves of the opponent, and an ability to counteract them in a split second. The log roll was quite a spectacle—always good for some laughs. But the requirement for winning was always the same: to remain standing on the log.

That's precisely what's required of the Christian. God expects you to stand. Look at Ephesians 6 and count how many times Paul urges Christians to stand (see verses 11, 13, and 14). Must be pretty important, wouldn't you say? The Christian is to stand in spite of all the fancy footwork of the opponent. The Christian must stand in spite of all the twisting and turning and bobbing and weaving of the enemy. He must stand in constant readiness, prepared to overcome every challenge of the adversary.

Dually Equipped

My first pastorate had its embarrassing moments, but one of the worst occurred during the initial move to this new place of ministry. We loaded the truck and took off across the northern plains. Even though it was only a 1-day trip of about 350 miles, we had to stop to refuel about four times. Unfortunately, that was one time too few.

We eagerly anticipated arriving at the parsonage, but as I made the turn off the country highway into the small town that would be our home, I felt the truck begin to buck. Then it sputtered, coughed, and died. Oh yes, we made it to the parsonage—but on foot. Not exactly a grand entry. The impression we gave as we came to town was one of being too pooped to pastor.

Take a lesson from the truck. When that gas tank ran dry, all power disappeared. The truck could no longer serve us as a truck. To function, it needed a continual source of power flowing from the fuel tank. When the tank went dry, that was it.

Christians are somewhat the same. When Paul says in Ephesians 6:10, "Be strong in the Lord," he's literally saying, "Be *continually* empowered by the Lord." The number one aspect of the Christian's dual equipping is this ongoing enduement with power. There must be a flow from God to you. Otherwise, you will have no power and you'll be ineffective, unable to operate.

Besides being continually endued with the power of the Lord, the good steward has to be always wearing the armor of God. During 4 years in North Dakota I learned a great respect for the weather. When you step outside into an air temperature of 30 or 40 degrees below zero, and a wind of 25 miles per hour, your body is under attack. More than once, the windchill dipped as low as 100 degrees below zero.

Now, who in his right mind would step out into that sort of weather in only a swimming suit? Proper protection is absolutely necessary under such conditions. Overcoat, hat, scarf, gloves, on top of three or four layers of clothing, must all be in place or you're in grave danger. Likewise the Christian has to be clothed with spiritual armor to withstand the deadly attacks of the enemy. Stepping onto the battlefield of life in just a spiritual swimming suit invites disaster. You've got to be prepared.

Remember what Paul has said so far: You must stand in the face of opposition from the enemy. That's a requirement for every Christian. To accomplish that, you need to be continually endued with the Lord's power and constantly clothed with the armor of God.

On Guard

October 1983. Beirut, Lebanon. Over 200 U.S. marines were killed when a truck bomb destroyed American quarters. Remember that tragedy? How could it have happened? It happened because U.S. troops were not prepared for such an attack; they hadn't taken the necessary precautions. They weren't alert; they weren't watching. Consequently, most of the victims never even saw their attacker. The secrecy and stealth of the enemy took them totally by surprise.

Paul says the Christian's enemy is similar. He's a master at stealth, an artist at secrecy, a genius at sabotage. He's also the father of sin, sickness, and savagery. That reflects Peter's claim that "your enemy the devil prowls around like a roaring lion looking for someone to devour" (1 Peter 5:8, NIV). He holds the power of death (Hebrews 2:14) and masquerades as an angel of light (2 Corinthians 11:14). Along with Satan himself are hosts of coworkers. That's what Paul's talking about in Ephesians 6:12 when he refers to "rulers," "authorities," "powers of this dark world," and "spiritual forces of evil."

They are your reason for being prepared. You have to fight against forces that are *personal*. In verse 12, Paul says we "wrestle" against these supernatural, super-evil beings. Wrestling means energy-sapping, hand-to-hand combat. It's a struggle with foes too *powerful* to overcome alone. The fight is against foes that are everywhere, far more common than we often are willing to admit. The Bible says they're present. You've got to be prepared. If you're not, their strength, their stealth, their secrecy, and their sabotage will overwhelm you—and you'll fall to defeat without ever knowing what hit you.

Round Up the Resources

When Paul wrote Ephesians he was in Rome. Not in some mansion or luxury hotel, but in prison. Maybe chained to the walls of a cell or to a Roman guard. Look at Ephesians 6:20 where he mentions his "chains." Whatever his precise circumstances, Paul was in far from comfortable surroundings. Around him every day moved the Roman soldiers. The clanking of armor, the rattle of spears, the clicking of hobnailed sandals—Paul knew it all. From what he saw as he lay in his prison cell, the Holy Spirit guided him to thoughts of the magnificent resources God provides for the Christian's protection.

The situation the Christian faces demands action: "Put on the full armor of God, so that when the day of evil comes, you may be able to stand your ground, and after you have done everything, to stand" (Ephesians 6:13, NIV). Catch the full force of Paul's words. You can't wait for evil to come, *then* try to prepare yourself. You've got to have the armor in place first. No warrior goes to the battlefield in ordinary clothes, and then changes into military uniform in the middle of battle. That's ridiculous! Put on the full armor, Paul says, just like a skilled

Roman soldier, then you'll be ready to stand your ground and fight.

Buckle Up for Safety

Buckle that belt of truth around your waist, Paul says. The belt, "girdle," wasn't really part of a soldier's armor, but it was absolutely necessary. The undergarments worn by men in Paul's day were bulky and loose, and the belt held them all in place.

That's what truth is like. If you don't bind up what's inside, what's under all the trappings, with honesty, sincerity, and integrity, then the rest of the armor will never fit. You'll get all twisted up, entangled, ensnared on the inside. The enemy will make short work of you because you've already started an inside job on yourself. Keep that belt of truth securely buckled at all times!

Then, position the breastplate of righteousness. The breastplate covered the body—both front and back—from the neck to the thighs. Vital organs were protected by it. If enemy attacks penetrated the breastplate, death likely followed. No chinks could be tolerated in the breastplate. Likewise with the righteousness of the Christian. What Paul means by the word "righteousness" is uprightness of character, holiness of living, moral purity. Take a minute to read Romans 6:13 and 14:17,18. In those verses, Paul uses the term "righteousness" the same way he uses it in Ephesians 6:14. Your devout and holy life functions as a breastplate in your battle with the enemy. Guard it carefully, care for it, protect it. Make a life of devotion, holiness, and purity a top priority.

Have you ever played golf? If so, maybe you've worn special shoes. A golfer wears shoes with little pegs in the soles to give him a firm footing when he swings the club.

Lots of people wear special shoes designed for specific purposes. Roman soldiers often wore hobnailed sandals. Like those soldiers, Christians need help maintaining a firm footing in their stand against the enemy. "Let the shoes on your feet be the gospel of peace, to give you firm footing" (Ephesians 6:15, NEB). With feet properly shod and firmly in place, the Christian is ready for whatever comes his way.

Douse Those Darts

"In addition to all this, take up the shield of faith, with which you can extinguish all the flaming arrows of the evil one" (Ephesians 6:16, NIV). American Indians may have used them, but flaming arrows were just as familiar to warriors in the ancient world. In New Testament times, coarse, broken fibers were tied about the tip of the arrow or dart and dipped in pitch. Anything wood, even shields, was in jeopardy. A leather covering on the shield, however, would snuff the flame.

Paul likens the tactics of the devil to the shooting of those flaming arrows. He uses every destructive scheme at his disposal to defeat God's people. He uses the flaming, piercing tongues of men. He uses the darts of disappointment, discouragement, depression, doubt, disenchantment—you name it, he uses it. The only thing that can deflect those devilish devices is that constant upward look to God that we call faith. Faith serves as a big shield to protect the entire warrior.

Take a minute to read the story of Elisha and his servant in 2 Kings 6:8-23. An uncanny ability to look beyond circumstances, surroundings, and uncertainty to the strength of God—that's what faith is. The story of Elisha illustrates this. Nothing the enemy tries against you can overcome your faith, because nothing can compare with the strength of the God you serve!

Hard Hat Area

Have you ever gone past a construction zone and seen one of those big signs: HARD HAT AREA? That sign is an attempt to maintain the highest level of safety in a potentially dangerous area. After all, the head is extremely vulnerable to serious injury.

The helmet in Paul's day was like the hard hat, protecting the head from attack and injury. Paul likens salvation to the Christian's helmet. Salvation, after all, is the most important item in the believer's armor. Without it, we're not even part of the Lord's army; we're on the other side. Without the helmet of salvation, we can't possibly win, because we're fighting on the losing side. Fasten the helmet in place by being certain Jesus is your commander.

Then take up "the sword of the Spirit, which is the word of God" (Ephesians 6:17, NIV). A sword is both a defensive and offensive weapon. With it, a soldier wards off attacks and inflicts defeat on his enemies.

The Word of God is a *defensive* weapon to ward off enemy attacks. Jesus used it this way when Satan came against Him in the wilderness (see Matthew 4:1-11; Luke 4:1-12). Peter used it as an *offensive* weapon when he preached to the multitudes on the Day of Pentecost. The bulk of his message was Old Testament Scripture, and Luke says, "When the people heard [his message], they were cut to the heart" (Acts 2:37, NIV). That confirms what Hebrews 4:12 says:

> The word of God is living and active. Sharper than any double-edged sword, it penetrates even to dividing soul and spirit, joints and marrow; it judges the thoughts and attitudes of the heart.

Without the Word of God, the Christian warrior stands

at the mercy of the enemy. It is the only offensive weapon Paul lists. God has put that weapon into the hands of His people and He expects them to use it. Check your stewardship of the Bible. Too often, Christians will drive miles to hear a well-known preacher or a famous Christian musician, but they won't walk across the room, open the Bible, and hear God speak. Practice using this light saber.

Communicate With the Commander

One final resource mentioned by Paul is of prime importance. No army succeeds in disarray, out of formation, lacking official orders. Someone's got to be in charge; communication must come from the commander. Paul lists prayer as the final resource:

> Pray in the Spirit on all occasions with all kinds of prayers and requests. With this in mind, be alert and always keep on praying for all the saints (Ephesians 6:18, NIV).

Through the communication line of prayer the believer receives his orders. He's told what to say, where and when to go, and what to do. Tap into that source of information. Don't just look to the other recruits for orders. Look to the real Commander!

God expects every Christian to stand against the enemy. The risk of failure is far too great to enter the fight without the proper equipment. That's why Paul says: "Put on the equipment! Buckle the belt! Put on the breastplate; take up the shield! Adjust the helmet, and wield the sword! *You*—soldier! God has provided the resources; now you respond!"

See the point? Paul doesn't say, "Go naked to the battlefield and then God will protect you." Not at all. You are responsible for putting on the armor. That's part of being a good Christian steward. Don't blame God when the enemy wounds you if you haven't put on your battle gear. The risks are too great to enter the battle without the provisions God has given.

Take a minute to check your armor. Make sure you're clothed with the protection God provides. If you're not, you're failing in your stewardship. The goal, Paul says, is to stand: "Put on the full armor of God, so that when the day of evil comes, you may be able to stand your ground, and after you have done everything, to stand" (Ephesians 6:13, NIV). The good steward's spiritual economy is in such order that even in the midst of severe testing and trial, he stands firm.

13

Be Faithful

"That servant who knows his master's will and does not get ready or does not do what his master wants will be beaten with many blows."

What's your reaction to that statement? Sounds pretty harsh, doesn't it? Jesus said that in a parable about stewardship. He asked a question, "Who then is that faithful and wise steward?" (Luke 12:42), and then answered it with a parable. The thrust of His message is this: The steward will be called to account for his service, so he'd better be faithful!

Accountability. Every one of us is accountable to God. Paul makes this plain in 1 Corinthians 4:2: "It is required in stewards, that a man be found faithful."

You expect the manager of the bank where you do business to be accountable for the way he handles money. You expect the mechanic who repairs your car to be accountable for his work. But do you see yourself as accountable to God? You are! "It is required in stewards, that a man be found faithful."

We Can Work It Out

No question about the principle. Scripture makes it clear that Christians must be faithful. The problem: jumping from principle to practice. "Don't give me theory and theology. Give me a plan to follow, something I can do to show I want to be a faithful steward."

Understand one thing right now: No book can spell out exactly and totally what God wants from you personally. It can offer only general scriptural requirements for which all Christians are responsible.

Think of it like an assembly line. I'll never forget visiting an automobile assembly line in St. Louis. Everybody performed his or her responsibility with amazing skill and regularity. As those cars moved along, one fellow put in bolts, another lowered engine parts into place, and so on, until a finished product rolled off the assembly line. Each worker had a different task to perform, but they were all working together to create one finished product. *Every* worker was accountable to perform his assignment correctly and faithfully as the car passed his station. Some things were required of all workers; other more specific duties were required only of certain ones.

That's the way it is with Christians. Not every believer is called to be a pastor or an evangelist. But every believer is to be faithful in carrying out the specific tasks God assigns him. There's no way I can spell out the specific tasks God has for you, but I can outline several scriptural requirements for which all Christian stewards are responsible. It takes faithfulness in both general and specific responsibilities to bring about what God desires.

The Call to All

Scripture sends out a call to all believers to maintain faithfulness in several areas. First, "Study to show thyself approved unto God, a workman that needeth not to be ashamed" (2 Timothy 2:15). When Paul penned those words, he was writing from years of experience in ministry to a beginning pastor named Timothy. The crux of

117

Paul's communication in both 1 and 2 Timothy is this: How can Timothy become the man God desires him to be? Among the most prominent requirements is the call to study. Lack of conscientious preparation means lack of approval by God. It could also mean slow spiritual suicide. Through the prophet Hosea, God observed, "My people are destroyed from lack of knowledge" (4:6, NIV). Study of God's Word is an act of self-preservation.

The Early Church began with study (Acts 2:42). However, not all of them studied well. The believers in Berea received commendation for their study over that of the Thessalonians (Acts 17:10,11). How's the stewardship of your study? Do you deserve commendation? Do you have a regular, preferably daily, program of Bible reading and study? Are you faithful to the educational program of your church? Is the time you spend studying God's Word sufficient when compared with the time you devote to hobbies, entertainment, and other such pursuits?

How about money matters? There's no way around it, money matters! The proper handling of money and material wealth is a vital aspect of scriptural stewardship. Remember Jesus said, "Where your treasure is, there will your heart be also" (Matthew 6:21).

When a man and woman marry, they usually exchange rings. Now those rings aren't that important in themselves. What matters is what those rings stand for. They represent a total commitment of the partners to one another. The tithe is something like that. In itself, it's not that important. But through it, the Christian expresses his commitment to the scriptural truth that everything belongs to God. If you keep back that tithe from God, you're no better than a robber and a thief! (See Malachi 3:8.) And every robber and thief needs to repent and correct his ways.

Maybe you've been a faithful tither for years. That's great. But remember God is also concerned about how you use the other nine-tenths. Paying your tithe doesn't release you from careful management of the other 90 percent. Take care how you use it, because it *all* belongs to God and is given to you only as a trust. And "if you have not been trustworthy in handling worldly wealth, who will trust you with true riches?" (Luke 16:11, NIV). If you fail as a steward of your finances, you may be disqualifying yourself for certain eternal rewards.

Winning at Serving

My mother lives hundreds of miles away, so I seldom have the opportunity to talk with her. When she visits, I invariably receive a kind, loving, motherly reprimand for not having kept her abreast of the good things happening in my life. Admittedly, I'm guilty. I fail when it comes to sharing my good news with her.

Many believers are guilty of not sharing the good news about Jesus Christ with those around them who need to hear it. Jesus didn't make this responsibility optional. He said, "Ye shall be my witnesses" (Acts 1:8). Everyone's a witness to something, but many believers fail in their stewardship of the good news they've received.

Listen to Jesus' words to the demoniac Legion: "Go home to your family and tell them how much the Lord has done for you" (Mark 5:19, NIV). You are to start there with your witnessing. Note the reprimand for those who do not. "Whoever acknowledges me before men, I will also acknowledge him. . . . But whoever disowns me . . ., I will disown" (Matthew 10:32,33, NIV). Be faithful in sharing the news of what Christ has done, simply as one who has experienced the saving grace of God.

Work at It

God redeems no one for a life of relaxation. He saves us into a life of faithful service. Every Christian is called to carry on God's work on earth. To repeat Peter: "Each one should use whatever gift he has received to serve others, faithfully administering God's grace in its various forms" (1 Peter 4:10, NIV).

In 1 Corinthians 3, Paul writes about working in the Kingdom. Everybody is expected to build. Work is not optional. Your work will determine your rewards. You may be saved, but if you neglect to do God's work, you will lose rewards. Paul told Timothy, "Keep alive the gift that God gave to you" (2 Timothy 1:6, TEV). Make sure that wood, hay, and stubble will not be your reward. Employ your gifts for God!

Forsake Not . . .

Stan would always station himself in the dining room of the rest home where we held regular services. He loved to talk, but every time I'd invite him to a church service or a Bible study, he'd brush it off. "Oh, I listen to that stuff on TV." Or, "I can hear that on the radio." His standard replies. He never did attend a church service during the 2 years we ministered there.

Perhaps he had lost sight of the true Church—that is, the body of Christ, that group of people that meets together as the people of God. God ordained all believers as His dwelling place, His temple. And wherever and whenever people gather in His name, that's where He is. When you do not attend church services, you may be cutting yourself off from the rest of the Body. You are risking malnutrition, a weakening of your faith. You are as much as saying to the rest of the members of Christ's body, "I have no need of you."

Hear the writer of Hebrews: "Let us not give up meeting together, as some are in the habit of doing, but let us encourage one another—and all the more as you see the Day approaching" (10:25, NIV). The good steward demonstrates his stewardship through faithful church attendance and support of his local congregation.

To Respond or Not To Respond

Jesus said, "If any man will come after me, let him deny himself, and take up his cross daily, and follow me" (Luke 9:23). Denying yourself and taking up your cross daily calls for personal action. Following Jesus—being a good steward of the trust God has given you—involves a *personal* response. To be a faithful steward, you must respond to the specific call God places on you.

God sends out a general call to all Christians to study, tithe, witness, work, assemble, but He also gives a specific call to *you*, to which you must respond. God places a special trust in your hands, then He says, "Be faithful in this calling." By all means, do it! James says it clearly: "To him that knoweth to do good, and doeth it not, to him it is sin" (James 4:17). You've got to respond to that personal plan of God; otherwise, you have sinned.

As you respond to God's call, you'll find yourself developing more fully into the person God wants you to become.

Nothing grips my heart like a person who is mentally handicapped. I remember growing up near a young boy who was unable to grow intellectually, unable to function adequately on his own. It was sad because the ability simply was not there.

More pitiful, however, is the individual who does possess the abilities and the opportunities to mature, to learn, to develop, but out of sheer neglect, apathy, stubbornness, or ignorance fails to do it. Churches everywhere are loaded with those kinds of people. It's not a modern problem, either. The writer of Hebrews scolds his readers:

> You have been Christians a long time now, and you ought to be teaching others, but instead you have dropped back to the place where you need someone to teach you all over again the very first principles in God's Word. You are like babies who can drink only milk, not old enough for solid food. And when a person is still living on milk it shows he isn't very far along in the Christian life, and doesn't know much about the difference between right and wrong. He is still a baby-Christian! (Hebrews 5:12,13, TLB).

That was Ken Taylor's paraphrase. Listen to how J. B. Phillips continues: "Let us leave behind the elementary teaching about Christ and go forward to adult understanding" (6:1).

Every Christian should develop in the faith, mature—grow up! Peter says, "Grow in the grace, and knowledge of our Lord and Saviour Jesus Christ" (2 Peter 3:18). Paul says, "Our people must learn to devote themselves to doing what is good" (Titus 3:14, NIV).

"That's all fine," you say, "but how?" Here are some simple guidelines to help you develop in your Christian commitment and, consequently, in your Christian stewardship:

1. Continually commit your life to Christ.

2. Practice regular devotions of prayer and Bible reading.

3. Worship with God's people every week.

4. Make Jesus the Lord of your finances and possessions.

5. Make your life a model of holiness and purity.

6. Make your home and family the center of your love, devotion, prayer, teaching, and time.

7. View Christian service as the privileged calling it is, not as a drudgery to be avoided.

Spell It Out

Seven specific areas are covered in this chapter. When put together, the first letters of each spell *steward*:

S—Study
T—Tithe
E—Evangelize
W—Work
A—Assemble
R—Respond
D—Develop

But that's not so important. What's important is for your life to spell *steward*. Be faithful! There's a reckoning coming. Every person is accountable for the deeds done in the flesh.

Belshazzar ascended the throne of Babylon as a gifted, blessed, informed man. But he ignored God and his responsibility to God. To him came God's words through the prophet Daniel: "Thou art weighed in the balances, and art found wanting" (Daniel 5:27).

Every one of us will one day be weighed in the divine balances. What will our stewardship show on that day? Will it show that we thought of ourselves as owners, or as managers, of our lives? Will it show that we clung to everything we had—including our lives—or did we hand it all to God?

Let us now vow to serve faithfully, to serve well, so that our stewardship will yield rewards when Jesus returns.

"Behold, I come quickly; and my reward is with me, to give every man according as his work shall be" (Revelation 22:12).